PAUL
The Worldly Ascetic

PAUL
The Worldly Ascetic

Response to the World
and Self-Understanding
according to 1 Corinthians 7

BY
Vincent L. Wimbush

PEETERS

MERCER

ISBN 0-86554-263-5

The paper used in this publication meets
the minimum requirements of American National Standard
for Information Sciences—Permanence of Paper
for Printed Library Materials, ANSI Z39.48-1984.

Library of Congress Cataloging-in-Publication Data
Wimbush, Vincent L.
Paul, the worldly ascetic.

Bibliography : p. 99
Includes indexes.
1. Bible, N.T. Corinthians, 1st, VII—Criticism,
interpretation, etc. 2. Asceticism—History—Early
church, ca. 30-600. 3. Asceticism—Rome. 4. Rome—
Religion.   I. Title.
BS2655.A65W56   1987   227'.206   87-11138
ISBN 0-86554-263-5 (alk. paper)

Contents

Abbreviations vii

Preface xi

Introduction
    Asceticism, Self-Understanding, and 1 Corinthians 7 1

Chapter 1

    The Relativizing of the World
    for the Pursuit of TA TOY KYPIOY
    (Outline of 1 Corinthians 7) 11
        First Corinthians 7 in the Corinthian Correspondence / 11
        An Exegetical Outline of 1 Corinthians 7 / 14

Chapter 2

    ΏΣ ΜΗ as Expression of a Model
    of Ascetic Behavior
    (1 Corinthians 7:29-31) 23
        ΏΣ ΜΗ / 23
        Proclamation of the Imminence of the End #1:
            The Address: τοῦτο δέ φημι, ἀδελφοί / 25
            The Proclamation: ὁ καιρός . . . / 26
            Parenesis: The Grounding τὸ λοιπόν . . . ὡς μή / 26
        Proclamation of the Imminence of the End #2:
            παράγει γάρ . . . / 33
        Provenance of Verses 7:29-31 / 35
            Gnosticism / 35
            Critique / 36
            Stoicism / 37
            Critique / 38
            Eschatological Prophecy / 40
            Critique / 41
        The Non-Pauline Origin of Verses 7:29b-31a / 44
        The Function of Verses 7:29b-31a / 47

Chapter 3

MEΡΙΜΝΑΝ ΤΑ ΤΟΥ ΚΥΡΙΟΥ
as Expression of the Goal
of a Model of Ascetic Behavior
(1 Corinthians 7:32-35) 49
  ’ΑΜΕΡΙΜΝΟΣ / 49
  Parallels / 54
      First Corinthians 7:5 and Jewish Piety / 54
      Non-Jewish Cutlic Asceticism / 55
      ’Απάθεια: Spiritual Detachment of the Philosophers / 56
  ΜΕΡΙΜΝΑΝ ΤΑ ΤΟΥ ΚΥΡΙΟΥ = ’ΑΠΑΘΕΙΑ:
      The Pauline Application
      of a Model of Ascetic Behavior / 69

Chapter 4

῾ΩΣ ΜΗ as Response
to the Urban Greco-Roman World 73
  ῾ΩΣ ΜΗ as Expression of "Response to the World" / 73
  ῾ΩΣ ΜΗ as Self-Definition and Pattern of Life
      in the Pauline Churches / 76
  ῾ΩΣ ΜΗ as Aristocratic Urban Spirituality:
      The Heuristic Significance of 1 Corinthians 7:29-35 / 83

Summary Conclusion 95

Bibliography 99

Index of Ancient Writings 111

Abbreviations

Ancient Writings

Aeschylus
   Eum. Eumenides
 Sept. C. Theb. Septem Contra Thebas

Chion of Heraclea
   Epp. Epistles

Diogenes Laertius
   Or. Orationes

Epictetus
   Diss. Dissertationes

Menander of Athens
   Fr. Fragments

Philo
   Fuga De Fuga et Inventione
  Leg. All. Legum Allegoriae
   Mut. De Mutatione Nominum
 Opif. Mund. De Opificio Mundi
  Spec. Leg. De Specialibus Legibus

Pindar
   Nem. Nemea
  Olymp. Olympia

Plato
   Apol. Apologia
   Crat. Cratylus
   Cri. Crito
  Euphr. Euthyphro
   Leg. Leges (Laws)
  Phaed. Phaedo
  Polit. Politics
  Prot. Protagoras
  Rep. Republic
  Symp. Symposium
  Theaet. Theaetetus

Plotinus
　　　　Enn. Enneads
Porphyry
　　　　Vit. Plot. Vita Plotinus
Seneca
　　Ad. Polyb. Ad. Polybius
　　De Benef. De Beneficiis
　　De Clem. De Clementia
　　De Tranq. De Tranquilitate
　　　　EM Epistulae Morales
Sextus Empiricus
　　Adv. Eth. Adversus ethicos
Sophocles of Athens
　　　　Ai. Ajax
　　Oed. Tyr. Oedipus Tyrannus
Tacitus
　　Agric. Agricola
Xenophon
　　Anab. Anabasis
　　Cyrop. Cryopaedia
　　Mem. Memorabilia Socratis

Early Church Writings

Clement of Alexandria
　　Paed. Paedogogus
　　Strom. Stomata
Ignatius of Antioch
　　Eph. Epistula ad Ephesios
　　Mg. Epistula ad Magnesios
　　Phld. Epistula ad Philadelphios
　　Polyc. Epistula ad Polycarpum
　　Rom. Epistula ad Romanos
　　Sm. Epistula ad Smyraneos
　　Tr. Epistula ad Trallianos
(Shepherd of) Hermas (Herm.)
　　Mand. Mandate
　　Sim. Similitudes
　　Vis. Visions

Tertullian
    Ad. Ux.   *Ad Uxorem*
De Cult. Fem.   *De Cultu Feminarum*
   De Mon.   *De Monogomia*
De Virg. Vel.   *De Virginibus Velandis*
Exhort. Cast.   *De Exhortatione Castitatis*

Others
    Barn.   *Barnabas*
1 & 2 Clem.   *1 & 2 Clement*
    Did.   *Didache*
  T. Naph.   *Testament of Naphtali*

Journals and Reference Tools

    BAG W. Bauer, W. F. Arndt, F. W. Gingrich, *A Greek-English Lexicon of the N.T. and other Early Christian Literature*
    BDF F. Blass, A. Debrunner, and R. W. Funk, *A Greek Grammar of the N.T.*
    HNT *Handbuch zum Neuen Testament*
    ICC *International Critical Commentary*
    JBL *The Journal of Biblical Literature*
  JRomST *Journal of Roman Studies*
    JThC *Journal of Theology and the Church*
    JTS *Journal of Theological Studies*
    NTS *New Testament Studies*
  NovTest *Novum Testamentum*
NovTest Suppl. *Novum Testamentum Supplements*
    SVF *Stoicorum Veterum Fragmenta*
    TDNT *Theological Dictionary of the New Testament*
  WMANT *Wissenschaftliche Monographien zum Alten und Neuen Testament*
    ZNW *Zeitschrift für die neutestamentliche Wissenschaft*
    ZThK *Zeitschrift für Theologie und Kirche*

TO

LINDA AND MOM

AND TO

THE BISHOP OF STOCKHOLM

Preface

This book is a revision of a dissertation written under the supervision of Krister Stendahl and submitted to the Study of Religion Program in the Graduate School of Arts and Sciences at Harvard University in 1983. A revision was in order because I wanted to indicate more clearly the importance of ascetic behavior in Greco-Roman antiquity as the background and context of discussion for any attempt to understand 1 Corinthians 7, especially, but also other early Christian texts that have to do with ascetic piety or social orientation in general. Such a framework of reference has been developed in connection with a collaborative research project that I am coordinating in connection with the Institute for Antiquity and Christianity at Claremont and the Society of Biblical Literature.

Words of gratitude are due many persons. To Ronald F. Hock of the University of Southern California and Nils A. Dahl, Oslo, Norway, for their careful reading of the manuscript and offer of wise counsel in many directions. To Virginia Hodges, Dora Otto, and Beverly Haumann of the School of Theology, for their speedy but careful typing of the manuscript; and, especially, Elizabeth Castelli, doctoral student at the Claremont Graduate School, for her expert typing of the Greek material. To research assistants Zachary Maxey, also a doctoral student at the Claremont Graduate School, Joseph Mante and Louise Sloan Goben, seminarians at the School of Theology, for their industry in researching, proofing and indexing. To Dean Joseph C. Hough, Jr., President Richard Cain, and the Board of Trustees of the School of Theology at Claremont for their moral and financial support for this undertaking and for their general support for the development of young faculty members at STC. To the American Council of Learned Societies for its supplementary financial support for the research leave that allowed time and space and travel for the completion of this manuscript.

Special words of gratitude are also due—to my thesis advisor Krister Stendahl, now Bishop of Stockholm, for his friendship and collegiality and, especially, for that for which he is legendary—his "hard" questions; with them I continue to wrestle. To my mother, for her love and support and faith—from the beginning. And to my wife Linda, for her love, support, and faith, but also for her endless patience in coping with my ascetic behavior in connection with the writing of the manuscript.

Introduction:
Ascetic Behavior,
Self-Understanding,
and 1 Corinthians 7

Research on "asceticism" in Greek and Roman antiquity has generally focused on the history of praxis, and assumed that common "ascetic"
practices reflected influence or borrowing.[1] It has been commonly thought
that early Christianity, for example, was innocent of "ascetic" influence
until it sold its heritage for Greek pottage. Both the focus of research and
its reigning assumptions were unfortunate: the former, because it failed to
reflect the understanding that critical to any discussion about what is constitutive of, or basic to, religious tradition is not type of ritual or piety or
language in itself, but *function* and *meaning;* the latter, because they failed
to reflect the understanding that notwithstanding the Hellenic origin of the
term ἄσκησις by which "asceticism" has been labeled as phenomenon—
both within the literature of antiquity and by modern classicists, theologians, and historians of religion[2]—it was Panhellenic and Panhellenistic
and enjoyed diversity and development.

"Asceticism" can be delimited by reference neither to a particular
praxis in isolation, nor to a particular *motive* or set of motives in isolation
from a particular praxis; praxis and motive must be viewed together to jus-

---

[1]See David R. Cartlidge, "Competing Theologies in Early Christian Asceticism" (Th.D.
dissertation, Harvard University, 1969) ch. 1, for a survey of the history of scholarship.

[2]In antiquity the Greek term had three fairly distinct meanings, as reference to (a) practice or training, especially of the athlete (cf. *Rep.* VII, 518E; *Polit.* 294D); (b) practice *of*
or *in* a thing—as of ἀρετῆς (cf. Xen. *Mem.* I.2,20; *Prot.* 323D; *Leg.* VII.791,B); (c)
mode of life or profession—of philosopher, anchorite. See Irl Goldwin Whitchurch, *Philosophical Bases of Asceticism in the Platonic Writings and in Pre-Platonic Tradition* (New
York: Longmans, Green & Co., 1923) 3n.1; James Hastings, ed., "Asceticism," *Encyclopedia of Religion and Ethics* (Edinburgh: T. & T. Clark, 1909).

tify the delimitation of "ascetic" praxis or behavior (as opposed to the more abstract term "asceticism"). The various forms of *renunciation* of all or parts of the social and physical world, which nearly all religions historically have enjoined upon devotees, should appropriately be placed under the rubric "ascetic behavior."[3] And recognition of the *universality* of ascetic behavior so defined should lead to a discussion of motives—whether certain patterns in or types of motives can be discerned in the ascetic behavior among or within various cultural and religious traditions. To make an initial generalization for the sake of example, the ascetic behavior (as defined above) found in the Hellenic world, or, even more broadly, in the Mediterranean world before the Hellenistic-Roman hegemony, was largely "cultic" in origin and character, a reaction to the threat of μίασμα ("pollution").[4]

Although ascetic behavior obtained in the Hellenistic-Roman period, it was different. It seemed to be a reaction not merely to the requirements of the cultus, but to an altogether different understanding of reality, of the self and of the world in which the self resided. Of the various explanations—historical, psychological, sociological[5]—for the "tone" or "change in tone" in piety and self-understanding in the period corresponding to, but not limited to, the Hellenistic-Roman period, none is more provocative than that of sociologist of religion Robert Bellah. According to Bellah, the "transcendental religions" emerged during this period in history. The cosmological monism of the old religious reality was being broken up and a different realm of universal, not merely cultic, reality was being discovered. This discovery implied and led to a devaluation of the empirical world. The latter was no longer accepted merely as a given within which one sought, through ritual, to fulfill religious obligations. In the "transcendental religions," even though rituals obtained, they took on new significance: whereas in the monistic religious communities rituals had been understood to atone for particular flaws or acts of perfidy, in the "tran-

---

[3]Emile Durkheim, *The Elementary Forms of the Religious Life,* J. W. Swain, trans. (New York: Free Press, 1915; reprint, 1965) 338; G. van der Leeuw, *Religion in Essence and Manifestation,* J. E. Turner, trans. (Gloucester MA: Peter Smith, 1967) 2:455-58.

[4]See Robert Parker, *Miasma: Pollution and Purification in Early Greek Religion* (Oxford: Clarendon Press, 1983) for the most recent comprehensive treatment.

[5]See Peter Nagel, *Die Motivierung der Askese in der Alten Kirche und der Ursprung des Mönchtums* (Berlin: Akademie Verlag, 1966).

scendental religions'' these rituals could only point to the more basic flaw
now deemed either human nature itself, or the social and physical world
in which human beings found themselves.[6]

Thus, what was now required was "salvation"[7]—from the self, or from
the "house" (σῶμα, κόσμος) in which the self abides. Almost universally
(Panhellenistically) "salvation" entailed some form of ascetic behavior,
namely, some form of renunciation of the world, or part thereof.[8]

Historians of religion and classicists have also pointed out what they
understand to have been a change in "tone" from more "primitive religion" to the religious spirit in the Hellenistic-Roman era. Gilbert Murray,
Martin Nilsson, Andre-Jean Festugière, Peter Brown, and others have made
note of the different (negative) view of the world common to both the Hellenistic-Roman period and late antiquity.[9] G. Murray, in the chapter entitled "The Failure of Nerve" in his 1912 lectures on *The Five Stages of
Greek Religion,* made the point most dramatically:

> Any one who turns from the great writers of classical Athens, say
> Sophocles or Aristotle, to those of the Christian era must be conscious of
> a great difference in tone. There is a change in the whole relation of the
> writer to the world about him. The new quality is not specifically Chris-
> tian: it is just as marked in the Gnostics and Mithras-worshippers as in the
> Gospels and the Apocalypse, in Julian and Plotinus as in Gregory and Je-
> rome. It is hard to describe. It is a rise of asceticism, of mysticism, in a
> sense, of pessimism; a loss of self-confidence, of hope in this life and of
> faith in normal human effort; a despair of patient inquiry, a cry for infal-
> lible revelation; an indifference to the welfare of the state, a conversion of
> the soul to God . . . an intensifying of certain spiritual emotions; an in-
> crease of sensitiveness, a failure of nerve.[10]

---

[6]See his "Religious Evolution," in William A. Lessa and Ezon Z. Vogt, eds., *Reader in Comparative Religion,* 3rd ed. (New York: Harper and Row, 1972) 39-45.

[7]A. D. Nock, *Conversion: The Old and the New in Religion from Alexander the Great to Augustine of Hippo* (Oxford: Oxford University Press, 1972) ch. 7.

[8]See Lohse, *Askese,* passim.

[9]The chronological perimeters are not clearly fixed. Analyses cover the late Hellenistic period to the third century of the common era.

[10]Gilbert Murray, *Five Stages of Greek Religion* (Oxford: Clarendon Press, 1925) 155.

In *The Gnostic Religion* (1963)[11] Hans Jonas argued that in reaction to the positive Greek view of the world emerged the negative, "Gnostic" view. In contrast to the Greek understanding of the world as the perfect exemplar of order, beauty, and the good to which human beings should submit themselves in obedience and imitation, the "Gnostic" was "inspired by the anguished discovery of man's cosmic solitude, of the utter otherness of his being to that of the universe at large." What renders this world useless—even evil—is the discovery of the other, superior world and the possibility of existence in it. As "Gnostics" find their true selves in the other world, "this world" is devalued.

E. R. Dodds (1965)[12] argued that the entire culture—including the early Christians—was caught up in renunciation of the world, in "contempt for the human condition and hatred of the body." The more extreme manifestations he thought were mainly Christian or "Gnostic," the less extreme in those "of purely Hellenic education." Belief in transcendence was thought to be at the root of this renunciation of the world: "The visible cosmos *as a whole* could only be called evil in contrast with some invisible Good Place or Good Person outside and beyond the cosmos."[13]

Although the historical, sociological, and psychological explanations briefly described above have undergone some modification,[14] a basic consensus remains: in the period in which early Christianity developed, a negative view of the world was common; the idea of the person and of personal salvation, or conversion, was emerging; that almost universally—again, namely, Panhellenistically—requirements for "salvation" entailed some form of ascetic behavior as renunciation of the world. To be sure, all as-

---

[11]Hans Jonas, *The Gnostic Religion,* 2nd rev. ed. (Boston: Beacon Press, 1963) 66-81; 241-53.

[12]E. R. Dodds, *Pagan and Christian in an Age of Anxiety* (New York: W. W. Norton, 1965) 35.

[13]Ibid., 13.

[14]See Ramsay MacMullen, *Enemies of the Roman Order* (Cambridge MA: Harvard University Press, 1966) 49-94; F. E. Peters, *The Harvest of Hellenism* (New York: Simon and Schuster, 1970) 410-20; 614-46; Peter Brown, "The Philosopher and Society in Late Antiquity," *Protocol of the Thirty-Fourth Colloquy* (Berkeley: The Center for Hermeneutical Studies, 1978) 1-17; E. A. Judge, " 'Antike und Christentum': Towards a Definition of the Field. A Bibliographic Survey," in Hildegard Temporini and Wolfgang Haase, eds., *Aufstieg und Niedergang der Romischen Welt* (New York: De Gruyter, 1979) II.23.1: 3-58.

cetic requirements or forms of renunciation cannot be explained by one motive. But it is difficult to avoid taking note of the change on the part of so many in so many different settings with respect to attitude towards the world—and ascetic behavior as an expression of it—in the Hellenistic-Roman period.

There were, of course, those individuals and groups not influenced by, or attracted to, the phenomenon described here. For some, especially those of the upper classes and their circles of patrons and courtiers, the Greco-Roman world remained a comfortable world. But for many outside the flow of power and privilege, without citizenship rights or a basic feeling of being rooted and "at-home" in the οἰκουμένη, ascetic behavior was attractive because, for one thing, it helped such persons and groups to articulate their sentiments about themselves and the world in which they found themselves.[15]

Again, ascetic behavior with different assumptions and motives obtained,[16] but what was new in the Hellenistic-Roman period was the popularity of ascetic behavior as an expression of disenchantment with, or a negative view of, the world. Of course, to say that ascetic behavior betrayed a negative view of the Greco-Roman world is not to say nearly enough. As there were different kinds and interpretations of religious and cultural experiences, so there were different "negative" views of the world. And it is important to recognize that all "negative" views of any world are nonetheless "worldly"—all such views are responses to the question regarding the most appropriate mode of being-in-the-world. Through ascetic requirements, through patterns in the motives behind ascetic behavior, self-understandings come into focus.

To the extent that interests in the history and meanings of asceticism in antiquity include locating the earliest Christians in such a history, to this extent 1 Corinthians 7 is of enormous significance. The chapter is not only one of the earliest of Christian reflections on asceticism, it also provides some of the clearest evidence—Christian or non-Christian—that ascetic behavior functioned to articulate orientation in the world.

1 Corinthians 7 has always been a special challenge for New Testament scholars and theologians. The challenge has revolved around two is-

---

[15]MacMullen, *Enemies,* 53-94; Brown, "Philosopher and Society," 2-11.

[16]See n. 8 above.

sues: (1) the origin or background of the Corinthian ascetics to whom Paul responds; and (2) the influences on Paul as he counters the Corinthian ascetics.

But perhaps it is precisely the premature preoccupation with "backgrounds" and "influences" that makes 1 Corinthians 7 so elusive. In the search for influences on 1 Corinthians 7, arguments have been constructed and conclusions drawn from inadequate or scant evidence, and the resultant understanding of the nature of the development of the ideas with which Paul and the Corinthians struggled is questionable. Efforts to understand ideas that "come into language" by recourse to "backgrounds" or "influences" are suspect because such efforts rest on the assumption that ideas remain true to language traditions. But ideas seldom rest solely upon, or remain true to, the traditions of the origin. They never rest upon "backgrounds;" they tend to move away from them, taking other ideas and presuppositions and motives along with them. They do not, as James M. Robinson quotes Günther Gawlick in the latter's discussion of the hermeneutics of language, "stand at the disposal of an experience as submissive instruments." They "must be taken over together with their historical webs, which then work over into their new area of activity, and . . . explode the monolithic unity of a system."[17]

First Corinthians 7 supplies us with neither the undiluted language nor the pure sentiment of the Corinthians. And it is very plausible that in this chapter we have to do *as much* with radical interpretations—literalist or spiritualized—of Paul's teachings *as* with any external influences or "backgrounds." Thus, it is Paul's sentiments and teaching that should *first* be the subject of interest. The questions raised by the Corinthians do not image a different "world" to which Paul stands opposed altogether; they represent struggling attempts on the part of a fledging Pauline church, in a mid-first-century urban setting, to come to terms with the demands of the teachings introduced by the apostle. There is little evidence of polemic.[18]

In 1 Corinthians 7, then, we are presented (least problematically for interpretation) with an understanding (Paul's) of the life of faith in the world

---

[17]See James M. Robinson, " 'World' in Theology and in New Testament Theology," in J. McDowell Richards, ed., *Soli Deo Gloria: Studies in Honor of William C. Robinson, Sr.* (Richmond: John Knox Press, 1968) 103; quotation from review of U. Wilckens's *Weisheit und Torheit*, PHR 10 (1962): 302.

[18]See the discussion below, in chapter one.

articulated as a direct response to questions posed. That the questions have to do with ascetic practices, that Paul responds to the questions as questions betraying concern about the most appropriate mode of worldliness, is important. It establishes the connection between ascetic behavior (or renunciation in general) and self-understanding. The ὡς μή exhortations in verses 29-31 are significant because they seem to represent a direct expression of Paul's understanding of the appropriate mode of Christian existence in the world. It would seem that there is a greater possibility for understanding not only Paul's view, but also the Corinthians' views, first through an investigation of Paul's views, their origins, sphere of influences, implications, and so forth.

The ὡς μή exhortations became a *locus classicus* for a large range of questions and disputes in early[19] and not so early[20] Christianity—far beyond the specific issues of marriage and celibacy. Thus, a history of interpretation of the passage should betray the diversification of Christianity from the time of the Pauline mission to the present era.[21] For this reason alone, it would be important to attempt to make some sense of the passage. But beyond this reason, it seems methodologically important to establish

---

[19]The references to 1 Cor. 7 and 1 Cor. 7:29-35 in early Christian literature are far too numerous to be listed here. Some of the most important references are in Clement of Alexandria (*Paed., Strom.*) and Tertullian (*Ad. Ux., De Cult. Fem., De Mon., De Virg. Vel., Exhort. Cast.*). See *Biblia Patristica Index des Citations et Allusions Bibliques dans la Littérature Patristique*, 3 vols. (Paris: Université des science humaines de Strasbourg. Centre d'Analyse et de documentation patristiques, 1975); J. A. Cramer, ed., *Catenae graecorum patrum* (Oxford: Oxford University Press, 1844); Karl Staab, ed., *Pauluskommentare aus de griechischen Kirche aus Katenenhandschriften*. Neutestamentliche Abhandlungen 15. (Münster: Aschendorff, 1933).

[20]See especially the works of Martin Luther and John Calvin, given their great influence in Western religious thinking. Luther's "Commentary on 1 Corinthians 7," in H. Oswald, ed., *Luther's Works* (St. Louis: Concordia Publishing House, 1973) 28:1-56, and his "The Christian in Society," in R. Schultz, ed., *Works* (1967) 46:260-320, have been very influential. Max Weber, for example, went to great lengths to point out the importance of 1 Cor. 7 in the West through its impact on Luther's thinking. See Weber's *The Protestant Ethic and the Spirit of Capitalism*. Talcott Parsons, trans. (New York: Charles Scribner's Sons, 1958) 84-86. See also Calvin's *Commentary on the Epistles of Paul the Apostle to the Corinthians*, John Pringle, trans. (Grand Rapids: Baker Book House, 1981). Much the same argument can be made about Calvin's role in making the chapter of continuing relevance among modern-day Protestants.

[21]More about this below.

clearly Paul's views before an attempt is made to decipher those of the Corinthians.[22]

The passage remains very influential in twentieth-century theological discourse to a great extent through Luther's influence. The Lutheran Rudolf Bultmann referred to 1 Corinthians 7:29-31 so often and with such consistency that many of his interpreters and critics have begun to summarize his theology by reference to the passage.[23] Oscar Cullman saw the passage as crucial in his discussion of "Salvation History and Ethics."[24] It has figured quite prominently in the recent works of J. Christiaan Beker.[25] Unfortunately, the tendency in the treatment of the passage in the works of these and other scholars is to hold the passage hostage to theological systems and programs. There have been very few detailed, critical treatments of the passage.

Wolfgang Schrage's article, "Die Stellung zur Welt bei Paulus, Epiktet und in der Apokalyptik. Ein Beitrag zu 1 Kor. 7,29-31" (*ZthK* 61 [1961] is probably the best detailed, critical treatment of the passage to date, but as will become clear below, I understand the import and function of the eschatological language quite differently from Schrage. Darrell Doughty's 1965 Göttingen dissertation, "Heiligkeit und Freiheit: Eine exegetische Untersuchung der Anwendung des paulinischen Freiheitsgedankens in 1 Kor. 7," is also critical, but does not focus on verses 29-31, or 29-35. (This appears to be true of most commentaries on 1 Corinthians and most studies on 1 Corinthians 7.) Gottfried Hierzenberger's *Weltbewertung bei Paulus nach 1 Kor. 7,29-31. Eine exegetisch-kerygmatische Studie* (1967), as the

---

[22]See J. C. Hurd, *The Origin of 1 Corinthians,* corrected reprint (Macon GA: Mercer University Press, 1983) 43-47, for history of scholarship on 1 Corinthians. I have in mind works, such as Walther Schmithals's *Gnosticism in Corinth,* which concern themselves first with speculation about the outside influences on the Corinthians, rather than with what can be learned from Paul about Paul and the Corinthians.

[23]See Schubert Ogden, ed., "Introduction," in *Existence and Faith* (New York: Meridian Books, 1960) 20; Dorothy Soelle, *Political Theology,* John Shelley, trans. (Philadelphia: Fortress Press, 1974) 8-9. For a complete list of Bultmann's references to the passage, see Bernard Dieckman, *"Welt" und "Entweltlichung" in der Theologie Rudolf Bultmanns* (München: Verlag Ferdinand Schöningh, 1977) 185.

[24]Oscar Cullman, *Salvation in History,* Sidney G. Sowers, trans. (London: SCM Press Ltd., 1967) 328-29.

[25]J. C. Beker, *Paul the Apostle: The Triumph of God in Life and Thought* (Phildelphia: Fortress Press, 1980); *Paul's Apocalyptic Gospel* (Philadelphia: Fortress Press, 1982).

subtitle suggests, is not a consistently critical treatment.[26] Herbert Braun's article, "Die Indifferenz gegenüber die Welt bei Paulus und bei Epiktet" (1967), is not a detailed treatment of the passage, but a generalization of it as a springboard for comparative study.[27]

With the exception of Braun's, the relatively focused studies of the passage have bequeathed to contemporary scholarly and popular reading of the passage the consensus view that Paul's counsel was directly influenced (thus also limited) by eschatological consciousness. I will argue that this reading of the counsel given in 1 Corinthians 7:29-35 is misleading, unless it is made clear in what way the eschatological language functions.

Obviously, there is need for more detailed, critical treatments of this significant passage. What is required is an attempt to isolate and clarify Paul's counsel as a model of ascetic piety in light of and in response to his "reading" of a different model of ascetic piety advocated by some[28] of the Corinthian believers. Such isolation and clarification can be carried out only if the models found in 1 Corinthians 7 are placed alongside other models from the larger cultural context. But such historical study can be carried out only with respect for the primary evidence at hand—the text. Thus, rigorous exegetical treatment of 1 Corinthians 7 is first in order.

Accordingly, this study has been divided into four chapters. Chapter 1 first places 1 Corinthians 7 in the context of the Corinthian correspondence, then provides an exegetical outline of the chapter in order to set forth the major issues and to isolate and establish the importance of verses 29-35 as Paul's articulation of a model of ascetic piety.

Chapter 2 is an exegetical treatment of verses 29-31 as the first part of the passage isolated (29-35). The origin and function of the ὡς μή exhortations is determined.

---

[26]Gottfried Hierzenberger, *Weltbewertung bei Paulus nach 1 Kor 7,29-31. Eine exegetischkerygmatische Studie* (Dusselfdorf: Patmos-Verlag, 1967).

[27]Herbert Braun, *Gesammelte Studien zum Neuen Testamentum und seiner Umwelt,* 2nd ed. (Tübingen: J. C. B. Mohr [Paul Siebeck], 1967) 159-67.

[28]It is likely that only the "strong," those so designated by Paul in 1 Cor. 8, are being directly addressed by Paul in 1 Cor. 7. Others figure in the counsel given insofar as Paul wants the community to be unified. But it must not be assumed that all of the Corinthians were advocating the rigorous ascetic piety Paul must speak to in the chapter. At any rate, the situation should not be thought of as a battle between the ascetics and the nonascetics, but between different models of ascetic piety—Paul's, the "strong," and the "weak."

Chapter 3 is an exegetical treatment of verses 32-35 as the second part of the passage already isolated and as the the Pauline reinterpretation and application of the ὡς μή exhortations as a model of ascetic piety. Possible parallels to, and influences upon, Paul's language and sentiments are discussed.

Chapter 4 provides evidence for the thesis that Paul's articulated model of existence in the world was respected in his churches, thus, in a rather significant segment of early Christianity. It also argues that the model is a response out of and to a specific social context.

A summary conclusion attempts to raise new questions about the continuing relevance of the Pauline model.

If ascetic behavior was as pervasive a phenomenon in Greco-Roman antiquity as evidence suggests, it is important for students of early Christianity to study the history of such behavior with a view to locating the early Christians in such a history. If it be true that "what one avoids, one condemns,"[29] given the enormous influence of 1 Corinthians 7 on the development of the piety and social teachings and orientation in the Christian west, it is important that the attempt be made to understand more clearly what Paul counsels the reader to avoid—and why. Given the present-day anxiety and confusion among both the religiously committed and noncommitted about the appropriate ways to engage the world as it manifests itself in the form of awesome political, military, and economic structures and powers, and given the tendency of many to fall back upon tradition and old landmarks, including old authoritative texts, for clarity and simple answers, not a little is at stake in an attempt to understand more clearly what counsel Paul has given. This study is just such an attempt.

---

[29]MacMullen, *Enemies,* 50.

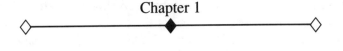

Chapter 1

The Relativizing
of the World
for the Pursuit
of TA TOY KYPIOY
(Outline of 1 Corinthians 7)

First Corinthians 7 in the Corinthian Correspondence

A certain consensus has developed regarding the position of 1 Corinthians 7 in the literary history of 1 Corinthians. There is relative agreement on at least four points: (1) 1 Corinthians 5:9 refers to an earlier (pre-1 Corinthians) letter ("A"); (2) 2 Corinthians 6:14-7:1, along with some passages from 1 Corinthians, because of emphasis on exclusiveness (10:1-22 [23]; 6:12-20; 11: 2-34; 9: 24-27 in order of certainty and consensus) may represent a fragment of this "earlier" letter; (3) 1 Corinthians 7-16 ("Letter B") was written in response to a letter written by the Corinthians; and (4) 1 Corinthians 1-4 ("Letter C") was written in response to the oral information about some of the Corinthians conveyed by a group from the house of Chloe.[1]

---

[1]See Hurd, *The Origin of 1 Corinthians,* 43-46, for a survey of scholarly opinion. Left unclear and without relative consensus is the historical relationship between Paul's response to the oral and written information ("Letters B and C," respectively). It could be

First Corinthians 7, then, according to the theory of composition adopted here, should be considered the beginning of "Letter B" written in response to a letter sent by some of the Corinthians.[2] J. C. Hurd[3] has noted six characteristics of "Letter B": (1) each topic appears abruptly, introduced only by the common formula περὶ δέ; (2) the responses are systematic, with a calm nonpolemical tone;[4] (3) the responses look toward the future—there is no criticism of the Corinthians' past behavior; (4) there are appeals to the authority of Jesus, scripture, common sense, custom, and Paul's own apostolic authority and personal example; (5) slogans from the Corinthians' letter are often quoted in order to qualify the sentiments contained in the letter; and (6) an appeal is made for mutual understanding among different groups having different opinions on the issues.

Final confirmation of the presence of all of the characteristics listed above can come only from a detailed exegetical treatment of the relevant chapters. But the presence of most of the characteristics seems evident from even a cursory look at such chapters. What begins to seem clear is that Paul was not responding to questions within a context of polemic or challenges to his authority, but was responding to requests that he reveal his mind on issues pertinent to the community's self-understanding and life. Since 1 Corinthians 5:9-11 indicates that the Corinthians had responded to a par-

---

argued that 1 Cor. is either the product of a later editor who brought together the originally separate letters "B" and "C," or that these "letters," although in response to different sources of information, were written within a short time of each other and juxtaposed by Paul, with 1 Cor. as the result. This latter suggestion would mean that the parties associated with Chloe and Stephanas would have met Paul in a period of time brief enough to allow him to respond to both sets of information in one letter. Since 1 Cor. 5:9-11 gives evidence of a misunderstanding of Paul on the part of the Corinthians in their reading of an earlier letter, the Corinthians must have received Paul's letter before either the writing of their letter in response to his (cf. 1 Cor. 7:1), or the departure of Chloe's company to meet Paul. This would clearly establish three stages in the exchanges between Paul and the Corinthians *before* 1 Cor.: (1) Paul's first visit to Corinth; (2) Paul's earlier letter ("A") to the Corinthians; and (3) oral information about, and written questions from, the Corinthians. 1 Cor. 7–16, *then*, is Paul's response to the written questions raised by some of the Corinthians.

[2]Cf. 7:1, 7:25; 8:1; 12:1; 16:1, 16:12.

[3]Pp. 65-74.

[4]Even 7:40b should not be interpreted (contra Schmithals, *Gnosticism in Corinth* [Nashville and New York, 1971] 234) as an unequivocal sign of polemic. Given the context and lack of other such remarks in the chapter, this remark could be taken simply as a sign of Paul's effort to commend his advice and strengthen its authority. Also, the possibility of irony should not be dismissed here.

ticular issue discussed by Paul in an earlier letter, it is not unlikely that they were now raising questions about issues and problems that Paul himself had already raised in that letter. Further, it is not unlikely that the slogans quoted in the section of 1 Corinthians beginning with chapter 7 ("Letter B") are the slogans that the Corinthians had taken from Paul's previous letter. If such a reconstruction is correct, it would mean that Paul is actually responding to requests to clarify himself on certain matters. Clarification may have been in order either because some of the Corinthians did not understand Paul (at least in terms of application in Corinth), or because Paul appeared, in the eyes of some of the Corinthians, to be reversing himself on the issues. At any rate, Paul seems to be responding to issues with which he was familiar.[5]

Since, beginning with chapter 7, Paul seems to be responding to written[6] questions from some of the Corinthians, the character, including the order,[7] of his engagement of the issues broached, is somewhat circumscribed. Nevertheless, to the extent that the questions to which he responds can be reconstructed, any excursus away from or elaboration upon such questions may prove helpful in clarifying, first, Paul's mind, then indirectly, the views of the Corinthians to whom Paul responds.

---

[5]Hurd, *The Origin of 1 Corinthians,* 240-88, supports the thesis that the Corinthians were responding to the change they noted in Paul's teachings as reflected first in his teaching during his first visit, then in his first (pre-1 Cor.) letter to the Corinthians. The latter, Hurd argues, represented a shift on account of the Apostolic Council and Paul's agreement to accept its decree. Along with Nils Dahl ("Paul and the Church at Corinth according to 1 Cor. 1:10-4:21," in his *Studies in Paul* [Minneapolis: Augsburg, 1977] 59), I think the Apostolic Decree thesis unconvincing.

[6]The part of 1 Cor. that represents a response to oral information—chs. 1-4—need not be discussed here. It is important to isolate the part of the letter of which ch. 7 is part. Dahl's proposal for understanding the function of chs. 1-4 in the total structure of 1 Cor. is convincing ("Paul and the Church at Corinth," 40ff.), but even he does not attempt to draw other than general connections between chs. 1-4 and chs. 7-16. He argues for chs. 1-4 as Paul's *apologia* for his ministry, as well as his attempt to counter what was considered *sapientia aliena, theologia gloriae* (the main tendency in Corinth being to anticipate the eschatological glory to the extent that nothing was left for the future). Chs. 5-6 should be seen as related to the controversies of chs. 1-4, insofar as they serve as transition from chs. 1-4 to answers to the Corinthians' questions. Dahl sees "enthusiasm" as the thread that runs throughout 1 Cor., and which Paul attempts to counter.

[7]But chs. 5-6 may belong to chs. 7-15. With these chapters, Paul may be anticipating the written questions to which he must respond. See Hurd, 83-84; Dahl, 55-58.

An Exegetical Outline of 1 Corinthians 7

Chapter 7 was provoked by questions having to do with the issues of marriage and celibacy as requirements for Christian existence. In responding, different categories of persons either already known to be within the Corinthian church or hypothetically posited by Paul for the sake of argument, are addressed according to marital status.

vv. 1-7 Married couples: the question of the purity of sex (ἐχέτω . . . γυναῖκα . . . ἄνδρα)

vv. 8-9 Singles who have not been married (ἄγαμοι), and younger widows (χῆραι): the question of wisdom of marriage

vv. 10-11 Married couples, both parties believers: the question about divorce

vv. 12-16 Married couples, one party a believer, the other not (ἄπιστοι): the question about divorce

[vv. 17-24 Statement of general principle: μενέτω ("remain"), with analogies]

vv. 25-38 Engaged parties (πάρθενοι): the question about perennial and rigorous celibacy

[vv. 29-35 Suggested model of ascetic piety: ὡς μή with analogies and explication (vv. 31b-35)]

vv. 39-40a Older widows: the question or remarriage

v. 40b Conclusion (to both vv. 39-40a and the chapter)

Paul does not appear to be changing his mind on any issue, nor does he seem defensive about his stand on any issue. There is some awkwardness on his part, as revealed in his tendency to agree with the positions with which he identifies the Corinthians, on the one hand, and in his carefulness to qualify his agreement, on the other hand.[8] He seems to anticipate the confusion that his responses might cause the readers, so he attempts to clarify himself by placing the specific issues broached by the Corinthians in a wider context of discussion (vv. 17-24). This is accomplished by using analogies that neither he nor the Corinthians had mentioned in the same context of discussion. In this way he hoped to make clear how the specific issues about which the Corinthians wrote fit into the whole of Christian existence. Since at one point he was advising married couples *against* re-

---

[8]Note: καλόν . . . δέ, 7:1, 2; 7:8, 9; 7:25, 28.

nunciation of sexual relations (vv. 1-7), *against* divorce (v. 10) unless an unbelieving partner desires it (v. 15), Paul probably thought it would be surmised by his readers that his position was basically "worldly." But since at another point he seemed to be advising (the widows and singles and engaged parties) against marriage (vv. 8, 11, 26), he thought it would be concluded by some of his readers that he was in favor of an ascetic mode of Christian existence. Verses 17-24[9] serves to make clear the principle that stands behind the advice given to each category addressed.[10]

Although it is clear that for Paul the single celibate life is "good,"[11] or an appropriate, befitting mode of existence, he refuses to allow this mode of existence, or any other state or condition in which one happens to be when called into faith,[12] to be a determinant factor in the legitimacy of ex-

---

[9]Note: μενέτω in v. 20 and v. 24 recall μείνωσιν in v. 8, and μενέτω in v. 11; κέκληκεν in v. 17 and ἐκλήθη in v. 24 mark an *inclusio*.

[10]Note: ἀδελφοί, v. 24; also, 10:1; 12:1; 15:1, 50; 16:15—direct address to the entire church. Even if leaders are being addressed, the entire church is indirectly in mind.

[11]Cf. vv. 7, 8, 27, 40a; also καλόν in vv. 1, 8, 26; κρεῖσσον in v. 38; μακαριωτέρα in 40a. After a brief discussion of the uses of καλός in the classical Greek world, Hellenism, LXX and Judaism, and the NT (including Paul), Walter Grundmann (Καλός, *TDNT* 3:536-49), concludes that no one precise use can be distinguished in Paul. The expression καλός (+ inf.) in 1 Cor. 7 refers to that which is "right," "good," "praiseworthy," or "valuable." Hurd, 158-63 however, first divides the modern scholarly conclusions about the meaning of the term in 1 Cor. into four categories: (1) ulititarian and pragmatic (no moral sense); (2) moral "good," one "good" among several "goods"; (3) the goal of morality, the highest member of a series of "lesser good"; (4) an absolute or ethical conduct beside which no other behavior can be called "good"—and then argues for his category #3. He argues for #3 because he sees the first two options as attempts at harmonizing 1 Cor. 7 with other passages (e.g., 1 Cor. 11:3; also Col. 3:18, 19, Eph. 5:21-33) in order to distance Paul from ascetic views of marriage. Position 4 is quickly cast aside as a special pleading on the part of two rather unrepresentative individuals—Tertullian (*De Mon.*) and Jerome ("Adversus Jovinianum" I,7). But #3 seems to overstate the case that Paul tries to make in 1 Cor. 7. He tries to avoid establishing any real hierarchy of values according to marriage and celibacy. He struggles to indicate the legitimacy of different modes of existence in the world. Thus, he argues that there *are* "goods," namely, there is more than one appropriate mode of existence in the world for the Christian. What is important in determining which "good" is best for an individual are circumstance and gifts from God. Thus, the term in 1 Cor. 7 should be taken as pragmatic and ulititarian (Hurd's arguments notwithstanding) up to the point at which πυροῦσθαι, or something similar, threatens. At this point, the hierarchy of value is established: both marriage and celibacy are superior to πυροῦσθαι.

[12]S. Scott Bartchy (*Mallon Chresai: First Century Slavery and the Interpretation of 1*

istence in faith—ἡ περιτομὴ οὐδέν ἐστιν καὶ ἡ ἀκροβυστία οὐδέν ἐστιν, ἀλλὰ τήρησις ἐντολῶν θεοῦ. ("Circumcision is nothing and uncircumcision is nothing, but what counts is keeping the commandments of God," v. 19). Up to this point, reasons are not supplied for the basis on which the specific categories of persons are addressed. But in verse 19 can be seen the view from which Paul sees the issues raised: marriage, single life, being engaged, or widowed—these are all "worldly" statuses. They have in themselves no power as far as Christian existence is concerned. Like circumcision or uncircumcision, like slavery or freedom, these conditions in the world do not determine status with God (παρὰ θεῷ, v. 24). The advice, then—μενέτω ("remain"). "Remain in whichever worldly condition you find yourself, since worldly conditions or status cannot commend to or separate from God." This advice was meant to counter what Paul took to be the Corinthians' antiworldly understanding of Christian existence. It was not so much the case that Paul's position was totally opposed to that of the Corinthians; he was not altogether positively disposed to the world; he seemed to share some misgivings about the world, but not to the same degree, and not for the same reasons.

"Remain" was not intended to support the *status quo;* it was designed only to *relativize* the importance of all worldly conditions and relationships. Yet more important, even the "remaining" is relativized: those who are afforded the opportunity (for example, slaves, v. 21), or those who experience the pressure of temptation (for example, engaged parties, vv. 36-38), can change their social condition or status without having their status with God affected.[13] What Paul wants to emphasize is the *relative* importance of "worldly" relationships and conditions vis-à-vis Christian faith and existence. He must argue consistently for the wisdom of "remaining" in chapter 7 only because the Corinthians, he thinks, have come to under-

---

Cor. 7:21 [Missoula MT: SBL, 1973] 132-55) argues that κλῆσις in 7:17, 20 and 24 refers to "calling from God in Christ," not social status or condition. But given the use of the verb μενεῖν throughout the chapter (vv. 8, 11, 28, 40a) in connection with the Corinthians' apparent desire to change social status or condition in order to effect a greater spiritual power or status with God, it is likely that the verb is being used in v. 20 in connection with κλῆσις in the same manner. At any rate, given the use of κλῆσις in 1:26, where it is clear that Paul refers to social statuses *in order* to make a point about the "calling from God in Christ," it is clear how intertwined the meanings are in Paul. Given what he understands to be the position of some of the Corinthians, the question of change must refer *concretely* to social status or condition, even as such change would effect one's status with God.

[13]See Bartchy, ibid., chs. 2 and 3, for a comprehensive discussion regarding the issues.

stand Christian existence—that is, pneumatic Christian existence[14]—as renunciation of the world, marriage and sexual relations here being identified with the world.

In his response to the various questions, we are provided a picture of Paul the pastor-teacher at work, attempting both to establish his authority and to be helpful by lending advice on some rather difficult issues. As much as he can, he avoids an absolutist position, preferring instead to address individuals or categories of persons according to their situations.[15] No criticism is leveled against any individual or group.

There are, however, indications of Paul's *personal* prejudices, his evenhandedness in the chapter notwithstanding. In anticipation of the discussion regarding the "strong" and the "weak" in 1 Corinthians 8, Paul appears in chapter 7 to assume the existence of two groups, divided into the rigorous ("strong") and less or nonrigorous ("weak") ascetics. Those who have the gift of continence (ἐγκρατεύονται) are counseled εἶναι ὡς καὶ ἐμαυτόν ("to be as I am," v. 7a). But those without the gift are encouraged to follow another, less rigorous path; this path, too, is "good." It is striking here that Paul, in spite of his obvious affinity with the "strong," makes it clear that the others lose no status with God (vv. 28, 36). Both the "strong" and the "weak" are in mind throughout the chapter, but the "weak" seem to provide the common denominator experience as the basis for the counsel to all categories of persons addressed.[16]

---

[14]It is not my concern here to attempt to establish the influence(s) behind the asceticism of the Corinthians, apart from what Paul reveals in his response. I accept as a working thesis some influence apart from Paul, but will not attempt to wage arguments about that influence until a clearer understanding of the issues as Paul sees them is gained. I see such understanding as foundational for further investigation into the ascetic behavior of the Corinthians. See John Painter, "Paul and the *pneumatikoi* in Corinth," in M. D. Hooker and S. G. Wilson, eds., *Paul and Paulinism* (London: SPCK, 1982) for a recent example of an attempt to clarify the issues.

[15]Cf. discussion above regarding characteristics of "Letter B." Also Werner Wolbert, *Ethische Argumentation und Paränese in 1 Cor. 7,* (Düsseldorf: Patmos-Verlag, 1981) esp. ch. 5, for Paul's use of authority in his ethical argument and parenesis in 1 Cor. 7; John H. Schütz, *Paul and the Anatomy of Apostolic Authority* (Cambridge: University Press, 1975); Bengt Holmberg, *Paul and Power: The Structure of Authority in the Primitive Church as Reflected in the Pauline Epistles* (Philadelphia: Fortress Press, 1980) 75, 82-86. The letters of exhortation, especially συμβουλευτικός, in Greco-Roman antiquity might provide useful parallels of a teacher corresponding with students about shared assumptions and ethical issues. But such an investigation is beyond the scope of the present study.

[16]Thus, the reason for the seeming ambivalence throughout the response to the Corinthians as expressed in the καλόν . . . δέ. Cf. n. 8 above.

To the married couples who have questions about the purity of sexual relations for Christians, Paul responds by saying that for those who have the gift the celibate life is "good." For those who may not have been given the gift and for whom the temptations of sexual immorality[17] may prove too strong, he advises the continuation of normal marital relations in mutual respect and consideration.[18] This situation, too, is "good" (v. 38). It is not considered by Paul to be an illegitimate mode of Christian existence; it is simply not his personal preference. What alone is argued to be an illegitimate mode of existence is the life of immorality (τὰς πορνείας, v. 2).

To the singles who have not been married and to the widows,[19] Paul responds by saying that it is "good" for them to lead the single life. Continence is "good"; but if the gift is not evident, marriage should be considered in order to avoid πυροῦσθαι ("burning," v. 9), in the same way that the married couples are encouraged not to forgo sexual relations in order to avoid the temptations to commit τὰς πορνείας (v. 2). It is not that the single life is superior to married life; it is argued only that married life is superior to πυροῦσθαι. The single life is "good," and married life is "good." The former is an option for those able to live the continent life; the latter is for those who either are not able to live the continent life, or—we may assume—choose not so to live. At any rate, again, it is clear that for Paul the only illegitimate mode of existence for the Christian is τὰς πορνείας (v. 2), or πυροῦσθαι (v. 9). Otherwise, both the single life and the married life are appropriate—"good."

To the married couples who might be considering separation, thinking it is a requirement for the demands of Christian existence, Paul responds

---

[17]Joseph Jensen ("Does Porneia Mean Fornication?" *NovTest* 20 [1978]: 161-84) argues that the NT usage of πορνεία includes wanton behavior, not excluding fornication. Cf. Matt. 15:19; Mark 7:21; 1 Cor. 5:9-11; 6:9; 7:2; 2 Cor. 12:21; Gal. 5:19; Eph. 5:3, 5; Col. 3:5; 1 Thess. 4:3; 1 Tim. 1:10; Heb. 13:4; Rev. 2:14, 20, 21; 9:21, 21:8, 22:15.

[18]I think I am in agreement with A. T. Robertson and Alfred Plummer (*A Critical and Exegetical Commentary on the First Epistle of St. Paul to the Corinthians*, ICC, 2nd ed. [Edinburgh: T. & T. Clark, 1914; rpr. 1955] 132) here, but they do not elaborate. They argue that Paul "is not dissuading from marriage or full married life; he is contending that celibacy may be good."

[19]In light of vv. 39-40a, it could be argued that in vv. 8-9 younger widows are addressed. Robertson and Plummer think, in light of 1 Tim. 5:14, that the younger widows are addressed in v. 9.

by saying that separation is strictly forbidden by the Lord. But if a woman has already[20] separated herself from her husband, she should either remain single or be reconciled with her husband.[21] The husband is also reminded that the command of the Lord applies to him (v. 11b).[22] Because there is a command from the Lord on the subject of divorce, Paul does not see the need to make use of any other arguments. It is enough that he can quote a command from the Lord, the relevance of which he apparently considers timeless for married Christians (vv. 12-15).[23]

To those involved in marriages in which the partner is a nonbeliever (ἄπιστος), Paul responds by saying first that he has no command from the Lord to apply to this situation, but he gives his opinion on the matter: he thinks it unwise for a believer to separate from an unbelieving partner, unless the partner desires separation. It was probably thought by some that the personal holiness[24] of the believer would be ill-affected by family life and associations. Paul emphasizes instead the stronger power of the holiness of the believer. No separation is necessary, since the holiness of the believer can not only neutralize the unholiness of the nonbeliever, but also protect the offspring (v. 14). The point seems to be that marriage and family life cannot be considered important enough in themselves to affect the

---

[20]ἐὰν δὲ καὶ χωρισθῇ, v. 11, is ambiguous. It could be translated as future ("but if she should separate") or past tense ("but if she has separated"). At any rate, both are exceptions to the command of the Lord. See David L. Dungan, *The Sayings of Jesus in the Churches of Paul* (Philadelphia: Fortress Press, 1971) 89, for a discussion of scholarly opinion on the matter.

[21]See Mark 10:1-12 and Luke 16:18. Only Matt. 5:32 introduces an exceptional case for separation. In vv. 10, 11—with χωρισθῆναι and ἀφιέναι—Paul appears to have made a distinction between separation of wife from husband and the putting away of wife by husband. But in vv. 13, 15 this distinction recedes. See Hans Conzelmann, *1 Corinthians: A Commentary on the First Epistle to the Corinthians*, James W. Leitch, trans., Hermeneia (Philadelphia: Fortress Press, 1975) 120nn.18, 18; Dungan, *Sayings*, 90-93; Albrecht Oepke, Γύνη, *TDNT* 1:776-89.

[22]The presence of ἀφιέναι notwithstanding.

[23]See Conzelmann, *1 Corinthians*, 120.

[24]I think Paul is here making use of the terminology of the Corinthians. They were probably thinking of marriage as that which could make the believer unclean or unholy, and of the single, celibate life as holy. Holiness seems to have been regarded almost as a thing to be possessed. Paul plays along with the Corinthians in picking up their language, but steers it in a different direction. This is certainly not typical Pauline discussion regarding holiness. See Otto Procksch, ἁγιασμός, *TDNT* 1:113.

status that the believer has with God. One can even remain married to an ἄπιστος without ill-affecting one's status with God.

To the engaged parties (οἱ πάρθενοι)²⁵ in Corinth, Paul responds by saying that he approves²⁶ of the celibate life, the life without the ties of marriage and family life, especially because of the present difficulty that marriage and family entail.²⁷ He emphasizes again the relative unimportance of the celibate life as far as status with God is concerned: one who has been single but desires to marry does not sin (v. 28). One who has taken a vow of celibacy, but feels compunction to marry, does not sin, that is, does not jeopardize status with God (v. 26).

To the older widows in the community,²⁸ Paul says that remarriage is "good," if it is to a believer (ἐν κυρίῳ). But he thinks that all would be happier (μακαριωτέρα)²⁹ remaining as widows. Here, again, the point seems to be that social status means little as far as status with God is concerned. To remain single³⁰ is to be happier, as Paul sees it; but not to remain single is not to lose any status with God.

---

²⁵The identity of the parties is still much debated. It is enough here to note the occurrence of the term πάρθενος on both sides of the digression (vv. 29-35), in v. 25 and v. 36. Even if v. 36 addresses a group different from vv. 25-35, they must be related in some respect, since Paul gives no explanation for a variation in meaning. In addition, in both passages, the statement is made that marriage would be no sin (vv. 28, 36). Cf. Hurd, 177-78; Werner Kümmel, "Verlobung und Heirat bei Paulus (1 Cor. 7:36-38)," in his *Heilsgeschehen* (Marburg: N. G. Elwert, 1965) argues for engaged couples.

²⁶καλὸν ὑράρχειν . . . τὸ οὕτως εἶναι v. 26. For discussion regarding καλός, see above, n. 11.

²⁷Ενεστῶσαν should be translated "present," given the manner in which the term ἀνάγκη is used in the chapter (cf. v. 37). This *suggests* concern with eschatology. But the reference is ambiguous enough to provide the lead into the eschatological argument in vv. 29-31. ἀναγκη is sometimes used to denote premessianic woes (cf. 2 Bar. 10:13; 4 Ez. 5:1-13; 6:18-24; 9:1-2; Jub. 23:11-31; Mark 13:19; Luke 21:23), and at other times to indicate distress not connected with the End (cf. Rom. 13:5; 2 Cor. 6:4; 9:7; 12:10, 1 Thess. 3:7; and most important, 1 Cor. 7:37!). See A. L. Moore, *The Parousia in the New Testament* (Leiden: E. J. Brill, 1966) 116.

²⁸Cf. n. 19 above.

²⁹Μακαριωτέρα, in light of the argument throughout the chapter, has no religious overtones. Contrast William Orr and James Walther, *1 Corinthians,* Anchor Bible 32 (Garden City NY: Doubleday and Co., 1976) 225.

³⁰Here in v. 40a it is clear that οὕτως (with μείνη) must refer to the more rigorous option. Here for the widows, it would refer to continued widowhood. It is likely also that in v. 26 τὸ οὕτως refers to the more rigorous option, that is, no change.

Verse 40b probably applies first of all to the advice Paul gives to older widows. Since in verse 40a he makes it clear that his advice has no higher authority than τὴν ἐμὴν γνώμην ("my own opinion"),[31] he has to make sure that his γνώμη is nonetheless considered worthy of respect. But the local application of the statement notwithstanding, Paul would no doubt claim the same for all of the arguments he had made in the chapter, insofar as the last argument is consistent with the thrust of the other arguments in the chapter.

Again, the thread that runs throughout the chapter is the counsel to "remain." To this counsel are attached different arguments used in order to persuade the Corinthians not so much of the importance of the *status quo,* but of the relative importance of all worldly statuses vis-à-vis status with God. "Remaining" is emphasized in chapter 7 only because it is the *Corinthians* who seemed to think it important *to change,* to withdraw from the world in order to enjoy status with God, more specifically, a higher pneumatic Christian existence.

With two digressions—verses 17-24 and 29-35[32]—Paul attempts to clarify his position. He makes use of analogies in both sections in order to place the particular issues about which the Corinthians wrote in a larger context of discussion. Like circumcision and uncircumcision, like slavery and freedom, liking having a wife, weeping, rejoicing, doing business— these are all, like the particular issues about which the Corinthians wrote, either worldly statuses or worldly involvements, and none of these has any

---

[31]Ἐμήν is emphatic, and implies the existence of other contradictory opinions, according to Robertson and Plummer, ICC, 167. But this is still no evidence of "opponents" with full-fledged theologies opposed to Paul.

[32]For the marks of *inclusio* in vv. 17-24, cf. n. 9 above. As for vv. 29-35, τοῦτο δέ φημι in v. 29 signals the beginning of a very important affirmation. Φημι refers not to the foregoing, but to that which follows. Δέ marks a transition from address to οἱ πάρθενοι to a larger group. Verse 32, with δέ, should be seen as the beginning of a second part of the digression. If only on account of style, a marker should be placed between v. 31 and v. 32; vv. 32b-34 compose two antithetical *stichoi;* according to J. Weiss (*Der erster Korinterbrief,* 9th ed. [Göttingen: Vandenhoeck & Ruprecht, 1910] 201-202), ἀμερίμνους in v. 32 and ἀπερισπάστως in v. 35 mark an *inclusio* for this second part of the digression, beginning in v. 29. This division seems to be consistent with the "a-b-a" pattern of thought which Weiss, 201, Bartchy, *Mallon Chresai,* ch. 4, and John J. Collins ("Chiasmus, the 'ABA' Pattern and the Text of Paul," *Studiorum Paulinorum Congressus Internationalis Catholicus* [Rome: Biblical Institute Press, 1961] 575-76) have noted. About this formal analysis see further below, in ch. 2.

relevance in the determination of one's status with God. What alone is important is the keeping of the commands of God (v. 19).

But the second digression goes a bit further than the first. Verses 29-35 interrupts the address beginning in verse 25, ending in verse 38. It is the subject of difficulty, or tribulation (ἀνάγκη) in marriage, broached in verses 26 and 28 in the context of address concerning the πάρθενοι (vv. 25-28), and whose immediate meaning and import are unclear, which seems to remind Paul of the difficulties traditionally associated with the End Time.[33] This provides him a lead into the digression beginning in verse 29. He takes the opportunity to apply the already traditional Christian conviction regarding the imminence of the Parousia to the other arguments in the chapter against a change of "worldly" status.

But already this particular argument distinguishes itself, since the eschatological argument can hardly be relevant only for the πάρθενοι. The eschatological argument betrays the significance of the larger pericope (vv. 29-35) to which it belongs for the whole chapter. In the context of the address to the πάρθενοι Paul not only supplies the most weighty arguments in support of his "remain-where-you-are" theme, he also proffers what must be seen in the context of the discussion as his counter-*model* of "worldly" existence to that model which he extrapolated from the Corinthians' questions. This "model"—ὡς μή—although apparently addressed to those among the Corinthians who appeared to be taking upon themselves the most rigorous pattern of life, was actually designed for all of the Christians in Corinth. It is consonant with the counsel to "remain" in that it suggests a way of being in the world, not of escaping from the world.

Verses 32-35 forms the second part of this second digression of the chapter. These verses bring to expression Paul's understanding of the *goal* behind the "model" expressed through the ὡς μή. As both *Paul's* counter-model of asceticism (vv. 29-31) and as his elaboration upon the goal behind the model (vv. 32-35), verses 29-35 requires detailed investigation. Chapter 7 cannot possibly be understood without some clarity about the function of this passage in it.

---

[33]Cf. references in n. 27 above.

Chapter 2

῾ΩΣ ΜΗ as Expression of a Model of Ascetic Behavior (1 Corinthians 7:29-31)

῾ΩΣ ΜΗ

Ulrich Müller[1] classifies 1 Corinthians 7:29-31 as an example—along with Romans 13:11-14 and 1 Thessalonians 5:1-11—of early Christian prophecy[2] regarding the imminence of the Parousia. Two formal elements—the affirmation or indicative element ("Indikativisches Formelement") and the imperative or exhortation ("Imperativisches Formelement")—are isolated by Müller:

Romans 13:11-14
a. vv. 11-12a—indicative element
b. vv. 12b-14—imperative or cohortative element

---

[1]*Prophetie und Predigt im Neuen Testament: Formgeschichtliche Untersuchungen zur urchtistlichen Prophetie,* SNT 10 (Gütersloh: Gütersloher Verlagshaus Gerd Mohn, 1975) 142-62.

[2]Cf. David Aune, *Prophecy in Early Christianity* (Grand Rapids MI: Wm. B. Eerdmans Publishing Co., 1983) for a comprehensive discussion of prophecy. The passage of concern here is located among prophetic sayings of Paul in basic agreement with Müller. But Aune calls for greater methodological facility in distinguishing prophecy from parenesis in early Christian literature.

1 Thessalonians 5:1-11
a. vv. 2-3—indicative element
b. vv. 6-11—cohortative element
1 Corinthians 7:29-31
a. vv. 29a, 31b—indicative element
b. vv. 29b-31a—imperative element

The parenetic elements, according to Müller, are more fluid in content, reflecting the different needs of different *Sitze im Leben*. The parenetic elements in Romans 13 and 1 Thessalonians 5 are seen to be suggestive of a baptismal setting in origin.[3] The indicative elements serve to ground or justify ("begrunden") the parenesis. Müller leaves the exact nature of this grounding unclear. The argument that the "end-time" affirmation was from the beginning constitutive of baptismal parenesis is suggestive, but Müller fails to elaborate. At any rate, he does not argue baptismal parenesis as the original setting for 1 Corinthians 7:29-31. On account of parallels both formal and thematic in the parenetic section, Müller compares 1 Corinthians 7:29-31 to 6 Ezra (2 Esdras) 16:35-44.[4] Form-critically, the latter passage is divided into the same elements as the passages discussed above:

6 Ezra 16:35-44
a. vv. 35-39—indicative element
b. vv. 40-44—imperative element

This comparison leads Müller, especially on account of the parenetic elements, to a further comparison of 1 Corinthians 7:29-31 with Jewish apocalyptic texts. The latter become important because they supposedly serve to link early Christian preaching about the End with Old Testament prophetic orations. In Old Testament prophetic speeches the subject of the indicative element, the affirmation, is the work of Yahweh in the imminent

---

[3]Cf. Rom. 6:1-11; Col. 3:3-5, 9-12; 1 Pet. 1:18, 22-23; Gal. 5:1, 13, 25.

[4]Sixth Ezra in the Latin version is 2 Esdras in modern English editions of the Apocrypha/Deuterocanonicals (KJV, RSV, NEB, TEV, etc.). The Latin Bible has additional materials at the beginning and at the end of 4 Ezra. The chapters at the beginning are sometimes referred to as 5 Ezra; the chapters at the end, 6 Ezra. The discovery of a Greek fragment of ch. 15 among the Oxyrhynchus papyri point to a Greek original composed ca. 3rd century C.E. by Christian writers.

"Day of the Lord." On the basis of this affirmation a summons or appeal ("Aufruf zum Kampf") is usually made to prepare for battle.[5]

On the basis of the parallels, Müller argues for direct formal dependence on the part of Paul upon Jewish (biblical and postbiblical) prophetic speeches concerning the imminence of the "Day of the Lord."[6] But the fact that we can find prophetic speeches in which are juxtaposed affirmations about imminence—"Day of the Lord," "the age to come," or the Parousia—and some type of exhortation, is not necessarily decisive for our understanding of 1 Corinthians 7:29-31. Müller's *historical-critical* arguments are interesting, but not persuasive; they remain too general to shed light on the history of tradition to which our passage belongs. A more detailed exegetical treatment is required before such results can be reached.

Müller's *formal* divisions of the passage, however, are useful. Using his formal division as a base, we divide the passage into the following units for exegesis:

1. Proclamation of the Imminence of the End #1: v. 29a
   a. address
   b. proclamation
2. Parenesis: vv. 29b-31a
   a. the grounding
   b. parenesis
3. Proclamation of the Imminence of the End #2: v. 31b

Proclamation of the Imminence of the End #1:
The Address: τοῦτο δέ φημι, ἀδελφοί

Τοῦτο δέ φημι is a clear signal of important, if not prophetic, speech.[7] And the presence of ἀδελφοί must not be minimized: As in v. 24, it serves

---

[5]Cf. Robert Bach, *Die Aufforderung zur Flucht und zum Kampf im Alttestamentlichen Prophetenspruch,* WMANT 9 (Neukirchener Verlag, 1962) for a detailed discussion of OT speeches. Cf. Jer. 46:9-10; 50:26-27; Joel 3:14-15.

[6]Müller, *Prophetie und Predigt im NT,* 170.

[7]Weiss, *Der erste Korintherbrief,* 197, refers to it as "*eine apokalyptische* Sonderlehre." Müller, *Prophetie und Predigt im NT,* 132-33, argues that this and other Pauline phrases (1 Cor. 15:50; Gal. 5:2, 16) function as introductory legitimation formulae, much like the παρακαλέω formula delimited by Carl J. Bjerkelund in his *Parakalō: Form, Funktion, und Sinn det parakalō-Sätze in den paulinischen Briefen* (Oslo: Universitetsforlaget, 1967).

to call attention to the wide applicability, thus significance, of the proclamation. Both φημι and ἀδελφοί suggest a rather abrupt change of address from v. 28 to v. 29, given the unexpected appearance of the former,[8] and the second appearance of the latter.[9]

Proclamation of the Imminence of the End #1:
The Proclamation: ὁ καιρός . . .

All commentators agree that the presence of καιρός is important.[10] It is often,[11] but not always,[12] used by Paul to refer to the period of time before the Parousia. Most often, Paul uses the term with reference to the divinely ordained and fixed time period that calls for decision on the part of humankind.[13]

It is said that the καιρός is συνεσταλμένος. Συστέλλω occurs in the New Testament elsewhere only in Acts 5:6, where it probably refers to the wrapping of a corpse in a shroud. With the subject καιρός in our passage, we should translate the perfect passive participle συνεσταλμένος as "short," or "shortened." What is referred to here is either God's shortening of the time of distress before the end for the sake of the elect, or, more likely, the traditional expectation of a short period of time before the Parousia.[14]

Parenesis: The Grounding: τὸ λοιπόν . . . ὡς μή

Hans Lietzmann argues that τὸ λοιπόν is lost between two sentences, that is, it is not clear whether it belongs with the proclamation, or with the sentence beginning with ἵνα.[15] Exegetes have lined up on both sides. Ac-

---

[8]Φημί is rare in Paul. Given 1 Cor. 7:6, 8, 12, we would expect λέγω in v. 29.

[9]Cf. v. 24. Again, it seems, in the context of vv. 17-24, to indicate the universal scope of the address—all members of the Corinthian church.

[10]Some witnesses include ὅτι before καιρός. But these are not the best witnesses. Cf. Robertson and Plummer, ICC, 155.

[11]Cf. Rom. 13:11; 1 Cor. 4:5; 2 Cor. 6:2; 1 Thess. 5:1.

[12]Cf. Rom. 3:26; 5:6; 8:18; 9:9; 11:5; 12:11; 1 Cor. 7:5.

[13]G. Delling, καιρός, TDNT 3:459-61.

[14]Weiss, Der erste Korintherbrief, 197. Cf. Mark 13:20; 2 Pet. 3:12; Barnabas 4:3.

[15]An die Korinther 1, 2, HNT 9 (Tübingen: J. C. B. Mohr, 1949) 34.

cording to Johannes Weiss,[16] if τὸ λοιπόν is taken with ὁ καιρός, Paul would then be saying that from this point (in normal time reckoning) forward (Weiss: "forthin") the "time" (καιρός) is short. But τὸ λοιπόν and λοιπόν in the Pauline epistles usually *begin* sentences, so what τὸ λοιπόν means probably lies *already* in the term ὁ καιρός:[17] it is ὁ καιρός that remains even to the present. Τὸ λοιπόν, then, most likely here means "henceforth," "from this point on," specifically with reference *back* to the καιρός.[18] It is the *remaining time* of the καιρός—which is traditionally thought to be short—to which reference is made in the statement beginning with ἵνα.

Since Paul has in the foregoing been addressing the subject of marriage in particular, καί has the force of "both."[19] It connects the marriage example with the other examples to follow.

With the subjunctive ὦσιν, ἵνα has an imperatival force.[20] It is based on the proclamation discussed above. Along with τὸ λοιπόν, ἵνα serves to indicate the nature of the relationship between the proclamation of the imminence of the end and the parenesis to follow. What becomes clear is that the parenesis is meant to be understood as following directly upon the proclamation: "Because the time before the Parousia (ὁ καιρός) is (always by definition) short, in the time remaining (τὸ λοιπόν) let those both having wives be. . . . "

Parenesis: 1 οἱ ἔχτοντες γυναῖκας ὡς μὴ ἔχοντες ὦσιν
2 οἱ κλαίοντες ὡς μὴ κλαίοντες

---

[16]Weiss, *Der erste Korintherbrief,* 198.

[17]Cf. Phil. 3:1; 4:8; 2 Thess. 3:1; 2 Cor. 13:11; 1 Thess. 4:1; 2 Tim. 4:8. Robertson and Plummer, ICC, 155. This might suggest already the beginning of a shift in Paul's thinking from concern merely about the delimitation of time remaining before the End to the nature of the present. Given the character of the treatment of eschatological motifs in this chapter, this shift is very likely Pauline and would support other arguments to be made below.

[18]But cf. BAG (1957) s.v., ¶3, for other possible readings; see also, Conzelmann, *1 Corinthians,* 130 n. 3. An inferential meaning of τὸ λοιπόν here is a possibility, although unlikely with the juxtaposition of an eschatological proclamation. At any rate, if an inferential reading is followed here, this would serve as early evidence for Paul's *reinterpretation* of what may have been traditional stereotyped eschatological prophecy to suit his purposes in 1 Cor. 7. Further regarding this, see below.

[19]Robertson and Plummer, ICC, 155; Weiss, *Der erste Korintherbrief,* 198.

[20]BDF (1961) ¶387 (3), ¶389; also, *JTS* 42 (1941): 165; 43 (1942): 179-80.

3 οἱ χαίροντες ὡς μὴ χαίροντες
4 οἱ ἀγοράζοντες ὡς μὴ κατέχοντες
5 οἱ χρώμενοι τὸν κόσμοω ὡς μὴ καταχρώμενοι.

Let those who have wives be as though they had none;
those who weep as though they did not weep;
those who rejoice as though they did not rejoice;
those who buy goods as though they were not to keep the goods;
and those who use the world as though they were not using it at all.

(author's translation)

We have in the verses above the second formal part of the prophecy as
analyzed by Müller.[21] Here the attempt is made, with the eschatological
affirmation as the base, or motive, to offer a model of existence in the world.
This is done by juxtaposing five examples of "worldly" involvement—
including marriage!—and five corresponding, suggested ideal modes of
behavior.

Several features must be noted.

1. The choices of examples of "worldly" involvement—with the exception of the first (οἱ ἔχοντες γυναῖκας) and the fifth (οἱ χρώμενοι
τὸν κόσμον)[22]—do not appear to have any immediate significance in the
context of discussion in chapter 7. They serve a rhetorical function. The
first example, concerning marriage, could have been drawn by Paul from
the larger context of discussion, or, as part of an originally traditional topos, could have made the selection of the topos for the context of the discussion in chapter 7 seem appropriate. That Paul makes use of the marriage
example among the other examples of "worldly" involvement—irrespective of the original point of its inclusion—betrays his understanding of the
nature and import of the questions which the Corinthians were raising. For
Paul, the real issue behind the questions is that of the appropriate understanding or model of Christian existence.

The fifth example, especially, whether of Paul or part of the traditional
topos referred to above, serves both a rhetorical function and more: it functions as an umbrella under which all the examples can be subsumed. Thus,
it aids in the effort to understand how the examples are meant to be under-

---

[21]Cf. the discussion above, pp. 23-25.

[22]Χρῆσθαι usually occurs with the dative in Paul: 2 Cor. 1:17; 3:12; 9:18. This occurrence with the accusative might suggest non-Pauline origin. This will be discussed further below.

stood in the larger context: they all have to do with engaging ("using" the world.

2. All the examples are represented by plural active and/or middle participles—with the article. Each example takes as its main verb the subjunctive ὦσιν (v. 29b), governed by ἵνα. Each predicate is represented either by the very same term as the subject (first, second, and third examples), by a related term (fourth example), or by a term with the same root with preposition affixed (fifth example). All predicates are constructed with μή, without article.

3. 'Ως μή is found in all five examples. This expression qualifies the relationship between subjects and predicates.

In *Koine* Greek the function of ὡς as comparative particle is dominant.[23] Among classical writers its function as conjunction is more marked. The New Testament, as well as the LXX, while on the whole following *Koine* usage with respect to ὡς, shows certain deviations and peculiarities. Syntactic looseness or greater freedom of usage resulted in some abnormal syntax. But the general meaning of the particle as a marker of comparison is, on the whole, retained. In our passage, the use of ὡς is a biblical—New Testament and LXX—peculiarity: the construction often found is εἶναι ὡς τινα.[24]

In our passage, since there is no second article (with the predicate), the exhortation calls for an equality or similarity not between persons in two different categories (those having x, those not having x), but between persons in whatever category (having x) and certain corresponding attitudes (being as though *not* having x). The contrast, then, "is not between two groups of persons, but between the actual situation of the persons and the way they are to treat their situation."[25] The comparison may be diagrammed as follows:

---

[23]Takamitsu Muroaoka, "The Use of ὡς in the Greek Bible," *NovTest* 7 (1964/65): 51-72. Cf. 56-57, especially.

[24]Some examples in the LXX are Gen. 29:20; Obad. 11: Zech. 10:7; in the NT, esp. 2 Cor. 6:4-10. For other uses among classical writers, cf. Herodotus IV.99; II.135; IV.81; IX.42; Thucydides I.21.1; II.71; Plato, *Gorgias* 517b; *Apology* 29a; *Leg.* 9p854E; Xenophon, *Anab.* V. 4:34; I.1.3. For further references cf. E. Mayser, *Grammatik der griechischen Papyri aus der Ptolemaerzeit*, Bd. 2.3. (Berlin and Leipzig: Walter De Gruyter, 1934) 167; BDF, ¶453.

[25]William F. Orr and James A. Walther, *1 Corinthians,* Anchor Bible 32 (Garden City NY: Doubleday and Company, Inc., 1976) 219.

Persons	Situation
". . . Those having wives	should be (=) not having wives . . ."

The Corinthians, whatever their worldly statuses or involvements, are being exhorted to "remain" where they are in the world, but adopt different *attitudes,* attitudes *associated* with different situations. But the vagueness of the ὡς μή expression forces us to ask whether it could not be understood— especially in light of the fact that an eschatological affirmation regarding the imminence of the Parousia precedes it—as a summons to *physical* withdrawal from the world, namely, from worldly ties and involvements. The examples of worldly involvements, as already mentioned, serve a rhetorical function, so they cannot *in themselves* provide the clue to the meaning of the expression. Marrying, weeping, rejoicing, doing business are all typical human worldly activities or responses to stimuli in the world. Just what was being recommended to the Corinthians in terms of ὡς μή in the context of chapter 7 is not clear. How could one remain in the world ὡς μή? Weep? Mourn? Traffic in commerce?—ὡς μή? How is 29-31 consistent with the thread of advice throughout chapter 7 to "remain"?

It could be argued that the change in type of predicate in the fourth (οἱ ἀγοράζοντες . . . κατέχοντες) and fifth (οἱ χρώμενοι . . . καταχρώμενοι) examples provides some clue to the meaning of all the exhortations. In the first, second, and third examples the predicate is the same as the subject, though without the article and modified by μή. Up to this point, it is not clear that what is being recommended is other than an attitude of indifference or apathy. But with the occurrences of κατέχοντες in the fourth example and καταχρώμενοι in the fifth, it could be argued that what is contrasted is not so much *degree* of involvement, as type or *quality* (moral, ethical) of involvement. Κατέχω in 30c literally means "to possess." Robertson and Plummer translate the term "entering upon full ownership," "keeping fast hold upon."[26] A negative connotation must be understood here, since Paul is advising against it. Here those who traffic in commerce are being advised, it would appear, to do so but without the attitude that leads to grasping and covetousness. Καταχράομαι, 31a, literally means "to use up," "to use fully." Here, again, because Paul is advising against it, a negative connotation must be given to the term. Here,

---

[26]Robertson and Plummer, ICC, 156.

Robertson and Plummer suggest, among other translations, "using it to the ground."[27]

But I think it no misuse against which the passage counsels. The primary concern is not about the ethics and morality of dealings in the world,[28] but about general attitude toward, and involvement in, the world itself, that is, concern about the world's power to entangle and disarm, to make one less ready for the imminent End. The concern, then, must be foremost about the *degree* of involvement in the world. But this means that the degree of involvement is a means to an end. The concern about entanglement in the world must be tied to an assumed value judgment about the world, as well as about what type of "world" should be realized.

In the passage from 6 Ezra (2 Esdras) mentioned above,[29] we have an important parallel that supports our thesis that the ὡς μή exhortations probably originated in a context other than 1 Corinthians 7, and that these called for a disengagement from the world on account of the conviction of the imminence of the End. It is the juxtaposition of the eschatological affirmation and exhortations regarding the response to the world in 6 Ezra 16:35-44 that makes it an important parallel.

> Audite vero ista et cognoscite ea servi Domini. [37]ecce verbum Domini, excipite eum, ne eis credatis, de quibus dicit verbum Dominus: [38]ecce appropinquant mala et non tardant. [39]quemadmodum praegnans cum parit in nono mense filium suum, appropinquante hora partus eius ante horas duas vel tres gementes dolores circueunt ventrem eius et prodeunte infante de ventre non tardabunt uno puncto: [40]sic non morabuntur mala ad prodeundum super terram, et saeculum gemet, et dolores circumtenebunt illud. [41]audite verbum, plebs mea, parate vos in pugnam et in malis sic estote quasi advenae terrae: [42]qui vendit, quasi qui fugiat, et qui emit, quasi qui perditurus; [43]qui mercatur, quasi qui fructum non capiat, et qui aedificat, quasi non habitaturus; [44]qui seminat, quasi qui non metat, sic et qui putat, quasi non vindemiaturus; [45]qui nubunt, sic quasi filios non facturi, et qui non nubunt, sic quasi vidui . . .

> [35]Listen now to these things, and understand them, O servants of the Lord. [36]Behold the word of the Lord, receive it; do not disbelieve what the Lord says. [37]Behold, the calamities draw near, and are not delayed. [38]Just as a

---

[27]Ibid.

[28]Contra Darrell Doughty, "The Presence and Future of Salvation in Corinth," *ZNW* 66 (1975): 71 n. 47.

[29]See above, n. 4.

woman with child, in the ninth month, when the time of her delivery draws near, has great pains about her womb for two or three hours beforehand, and when the child comes forth from the womb, there will not be a moment's delay, [39]so the calamities will not delay in coming forth upon the earth, and the world will groan, and pains will seize it on every side. [40]Hear my words, O my people; prepare for battle, and in the midst of the calamities be like strangers on the earth. [41]Let him that sells be like one who will flee; let him that buys be like one who will lose; [42]let him that does business be like one who will not make a profit; and let him that builds a house be like one who will not live in it; [43]let him that sows be like one who will not reap; so also him that prunes the vines, like one who will not gather the grapes; [44]them that marry, like those who will have no children and them that do not marry like those who are widowed.[30]

The exhortations in verses 40-44 emphasize the importance—in light of the conviction of the imminence of evils—of preparation for battle ''in the midst of the calamities'' (*parate vos in pugnam et in malis sic estote quasi advenae terrae*), of a sitting loose from all worldly activities and involvements. The things of the world are relativized; no one should continue to live as though life will go on as usual. Verse 44, regarding those who marry, is especially important for purposes of comparison with 1 Corinthians 7:29-31. Renunciation of married life is not advised, but the avoidance of more entanglements, more worldly responsibilities in the context of marriage, for example, children, is advised. This is instructive; the *motive* behind the exhortations in 6 Ezra 16:40-44 appears to be similar to the motive behind the exhortations in 1 Corinthians 7:29-31. But because of the larger context of discussion in 1 Corinthians 7, this motive seems to have less significance. It is clear that the motive behind the exhortations in 6 Ezra is the conviction of the immence of distress and evil upon the earth (vv. 37-39). The question of the essential moral and ethical worth of the world itself, of marriage, commerce, and so forth, is not obtained.

The imminence motif, to be sure, is present in 1 Corinthians 7:29-31, but it is not so clearly the single motive behind the exhortations in the larger context of the chapter. Paul argues throughout chapter 7 that one's condition or status in the world has no power to affect for good or ill status

---

[30]The Latin text is from Otto Fritzsche, ed., *Libri Apocryphi Veteris Testamenti Graece* (Leipzig: Brockhaus, 1871). The English translation is by Bruce M. Metzger in *The Old Testament Pseudepigrapha*, ed. J. H. Charlesworth (Garden City: Doubleday, 1983). Note differences in verse division between the Latin text and English translation. The verse divisions of the latter are followed here.

with God. Because worldly statuses or conditions mean nothing with respect to status with God, as well as because the End is near, all should remain in whatever worldly condition they were in when they were called by
God. Also, because the world means nothing as far as status with God is
concerned, one should respond to the world as though it were ἀδιάφορον,
that is, one should sit loose from it.

What seemed of importance to Paul in terms of his answering the Corinthians' questions was not so much the eschatological affirmation as the
emphasis on the relativizing of worldly things, which comes to expression
in the ὡς μή exhortations. The eschatological affirmation is not developed.
This might suggest that 1 Corinthians 7:29b-31a did not originate with Paul,
but was employed by him in order to commend the model of response to
the world which he thought appropriate in attempting to answer the Corinthians' questions.

Our suspicion about the non-Pauline origin of verses 29b-31a is
heightened by the important parallel in 6 Ezra. The latter provides an example of the same pattern of expression of similar motifs in a *Sitz im Leben*
different from that which lies behind 1 Corinthians 7, but which could
square rather easily with verses 29b-31a in isolation. Given the fact that
the other NT allusions in 6 Ezra point away from Pauline influence and
more in the direction of apocalypticism, and given Paul's attempt in verses
31b-35 to reinterpret the significance of the eschatological affirmation in
verse 29a, we are forced to ask whether verses 29b-31a could not have
originated in a *Sitz im Leben* different from 1 Corinthians 7, perhaps, more
similar to that reflected in 6 Ezra 16. This will be discussed further below.

Proclamation of the Imminence the End #2:
παράγει γάρ . . .

This proclamation not only supplies, in conjunction with verse 29a, at
least the apparent reason for the ὡς μή exhortations; it also indicates that
which Paul has in mind throughout his response to the questions raised by
the Corinthians. It seems clear that it is ὁ κόσμος οὗτος ("this world")
with which the Corinthians' questions have to do. The κόσμος in which
the shortened time is playing itself out is ὁ κόσμος οὗτος, and as such,
has elements and concerns (σχῆμα) that are impermanent (παράγει).
Those things that belong naturally to ὁ κόσμος οὗτος are not in this context deemed evil in themselves; they are simply transient and, as such, not
worthy of serious commitment. The shortness of the time remaining be-

fore the end is not emphasized here. In point of fact, it is not the κόσμος that is said to be passing away, but its σχῆμα. The latter refers to the distinctive manifestations—institutions, morals, ideals—that characterize the κόσμος.[31] This language suggests some interest in social critique.

The question should be asked, why a second proclamation? Is Paul restating the first proclamation, or is he making a different point? We have already indicated the different emphasis in the second proclamation with respect to the imminence motif. This would suggest not so much a contradiction of the first proclamation as an effort to explain the manner in which the first proclamation is meant to be understood by the Corinthians. Not only because the time remaining before the End is short, but also because the world is ephemeral, is passing away, should "those having . . . be as if not."

What we seem to have in verses 29-31, then, is eschatological language employed in two different ways: Verse 29a emphasizes the *temporal limitedness* of the present age; verse 31b emphasizes the *ephemeral quality* of the present order. These emphases are not antithetical. They are combined in a prominent way in the Jewish apocalyptic literature of the intertestamental period (compare 2 Bar. 24; 49-51; 2 En. 66; As. Mos. 1). The future hope of the Old Testament prophecies become in the intertestamental period the doctrine of the morally and ethically dualistic "two ages," and of the transcendental nature of the coming kingdom. The Kingdom or the "Age to Come" is expected to bring with it cataclysmic, as opposed to evolutionary, change.[32] This change is expected always in the near future, because the present age is evil and tragic.[33]

What is different about the emphasis in 1 Corinthians 7:31b is that it implies, through the employment of the present tense verb παράγει, that the imminence of the End is no longer the focus: the concern seems to be to describe the *perennial* state of affairs in the present order. This statement was probably affixed by Paul to verses 29b-31a in order to make the

---

[31]Johannes Schneider, σχῆμα, *TDNT* 7:956. The term is found only here and at Phil. 2:7 in the New Testament. But Rom. 12:2 (αἰών) should also be seen as expressive of similar view. Cf. Weiss, *Der erste Korintherbrief,* 201.

[32]J. C. H. Lebram, "The Piety of the Jewish Apocalyptists," in *Apocalypticism in the Mediterranean World and the Near East,* ed. D. Hellholm (Tübingen: J. C. B. Mohr, 1983) 175.

[33]Cf. 2 En. 66: 2 Bar. 27, 49; 1 En. 10.

latter relevant for his overall purposes in chapter 7. At any rate, its very appearance justifies the raising of the question of the provenance of verses 29b-31a.

The Provenance of Verses 29b-31a

Nearly all interpreters of the passage argue or assume Pauline authorship.[34] But, of course, these interpreters differ greatly with respect to opinions about the influences upon Paul and the social-ideological context in which the passage is to be placed and interpreted. The opinions fall into three major categories: (1) Gnosticism; (2) Stoicism; and (3) Eschatological Prophecy.

Gnosticism

To my knowledge, only Hans Jonas—not even Walter Schmithals!—has argued for "Gnostic" influence in the passage. In both his *The Gnostic Religion*[35] and *Gnosis und spätantiker Geist*,[36] Jonas argues that verses 29-31 should be understood as an expression consonant with the acosmic sentiment of the "transcendental religion" of which "Gnosticism" and Christianity were a part. The new "transcendental religion" Jonas defines and delimits over against the classical Greek world.

The "Gnostic" reinterpretation of the cosmos had clear ramifications for a system of virtue different from that of the Greeks. Precisely because it viewed the cosmos positively, the classical Greek position of "identifying virtue as the following of the design of nature, as bringing nature's designs into its right, as doing the right things in the right way at the right time," was consistent. Because it was thought that this true nature could be realized only in interaction with other things and in a context in which other beings are found, namely, in the world, then the whole of the cosmos was deemed worthy of engagement. But because the "Gnostics" had no respect for the cosmos as a divine whole, they could not base a system of ethics or ideas of virtue on a positive engagement of the cosmos. Nevertheless, their idea of virtue nonetheless represented *some* type of response

---

[34]Besides the writer, only Siegfried Schulz and Wolfgang Schrage, to my knowledge, are exceptions. Regarding their arguments, see below.

[35]Second rev. ed. (Boston: Beacon Press, 1963).

[36]Vol. 2/1, 2nd ed. (Göttingen: Vandenhoeck & Ruprecht, 1966) 34.

to the cosmos. In fact, according to Jonas, their negative attitude to the cosmos provided some options with respect to modes of worldly conduct: (1) nihilism; (2) libertinism; and (3) asceticism.[37]

Jonas sees 1 Corinthians 7:29-31 as one of the clearest expressions of the "acosmic spirit." The following summarizing description of the "common spirit" of the acosmic anticlassical position Jonas applies both to the "Gnostics" and to Paul as author of 1 Corinthians 7:29-31.

> "[L]ooking towards God" . . . is a jumping across all intervening realities, which for this direct relationship are nothing but fetters and obstacles, or distracting temptations, or at best irrelevant. The sum of these intervening realities is the world, including the social world. The surpassing interest in salvation, the exclusive concern in the destiny of the transcendent self, "denatures" as it were these realities and takes the heart out of the concern with them where such concern is unavoidable. An essential mental reservation qualifies participation in the things of the world, and even one's own person as involved with those things is viewed from the distance of the beyond.[38]

Critique

That 1 Corinthians 7:29-31 reflects what Jonas calls an acosmic sentiment is clear. That the sentiment is similar to many of the views we can associate with "the Gnostics" is also clear. What is not clear, however, is the background of the acosmism reflected in the passage. That primitive Christianity can be associated with "Gnosticism" insofar as the former reflects a different, nonclassical view of the cosmos may not be as significant as Jonas suggests, so far as an assessment of the background of our passage is concerned. If the acosmism was a broad movement encompassing many disparate groups with different origins and motivations— "Gnosticism" being only one among the many manifestations—then our passage cannot be accounted for by the mere noting of the acosmic view that it reflects.

If full-blown "Gnostic" systems are examined closely, it will be found that different presuppositions and motives were behind their origins and development, the common acosmic spirit notwithstanding. Surely, given the origins and development of primitive Christianity in general, given the

---

[37]*The Gnostic Religion*, 270-75.

[38]Ibid., 268.

background and experiences of the apostle Paul, the acosmic spirit of "Gnosticism" as the explanation for the origin of the passage is inadequate and inappropriate. What is required is more investigation into the particular kind of acosmism that the passage reflects.

From the exegetical analysis of the passage, verse 29a (along with 31b) was established as the ground, the base, for the exhortations in verses 29b-31a.[39] It would seem inappropriate, then, to suggest an origin or background of the passage that could not account for this ground. Jonas's argument is not so much incorrect as it is inadequate for our purposes. It places the passage on a trajectory with which we are familiar, and that seems appropriate given the views the exhortations reflect, but whose points we cannot yet clearly enough match with the details of our passage. Since the "acosmic spirit" was broader than "Gnosticism," we must be more specific about the influences on the passage.

Stoicism

In all thorough discussions about the parallels between Paul's writing and Stoic teaching the concept of detachment (ἀταραξία) among the Stoics and the teaching regarding the Christian's relationship with the world in Paul are usually addressed. First Corinthians 7 usually figures prominently in such discussions because in it is identified not only language found in Stoic writings, but also the topos of detachment-from-the-world which preoccupies the Stoics.

Herbert Braun's article, "Die Indifferenz gegenüber der Welt bei Paulus und bei Epiktet,"[40] represents the most detailed discussion to date of the similarities between the Stoics and Paul with respect to indifference to the world. Braun notes that Paul and Epictetus do not use the same terminology to express their respective positions. Paul makes use of the ὡς μή language in the context of a response to questions about marriage. The ὡς μή is repeated and used to apply to all involvements in life. Epictetus makes use of many different kinds of language to articulate his position. No one phrase or formula captures his sentiment. Braun, however, taking the topic heading of *Diss. 3,* suggests that μὴ προσπασχεῖν be treated as

---

[39]Cf. above, pp. 25-26, 33-34.

[40]In his *Gesammelte Studien zum Neuen Testament und Seiner Welt,* 2nd ed. (Tübingen: J. C. B. Mohr, 1967) 159-67.

an umbrella topos for Epictetus's teaching on philosophical detachment.[41]
So Paul's ὡς μή is equated with Epictetus's μὴ προσπασχεῖν.[42]

Braun concedes that Paul does not simply replay the Stoic line with respect to indifference to the world. Paul's divergence from Stoic teaching
on detachment appears so obvious at points that Braun is forced to question
the wisdom of the employment of "diese stoa-nahe Position" in 1 Corinthians 7:29-31. "Denn seine Intention ist nicht die Autarkie der stoischen
Indifferenz, sondern das συν der ἀγάπη.[43]

As far as I have been able to determine, the only scholar to argue for
a *formal* parallel to 1 Corinthians 7:29b-31a in the Greek world is R.
Penna.[44] He argues for such in the words of Diogenes the Cynic as cited
in Diogenes Laertius's *Lives* 6.29:

> ἐπῄνει τοὺς μέλλοντας γαμεῖν καὶ μὴ γαμεῖν, καὶ τοὺς μέλ-
> λοντας καταπλεῖν καὶ μὴ καταπλεῖν, καὶ τοὺς μέλλοντας πολ-
> ιτεύεσθαι καὶ μὴ πολιτεύεσθαι, καὶ τοὺς παιδοτροφεῖν, καὶ
> τοὺς παρασκευαζομένους συμβιοῦν τοῖς δυνάσταις καὶ μὴ
> προσιόντας.

> He would praise those who were about to marry but do not, those who were
> about to go on a voyage but do not, those who were about to enter public
> life but do not, those who were thinking of raising a family but do not,
> those who position themselves to take up with the powerful, but do not.

> (author's translation)

Of course, Penna rightly acknowledges that irreconcilable differences separate both the content and function of Diogenes's words and 1 Corinthians
7:29b-31a. Paul's counsel seems to be not only less absolutist in terms of
the commendation of social ethical behavior, but also less critical of society. His middle ground resonates more clearly with Stoic teachings than
with the social criticism of the Cynic.

Critique

We may question Braun's conclusion about Paul's general "Intention" in the passage,[45] but his acknowledgment that the passage seems not

---

[41]Ibid., 160-61. In Epictetus, cf. *Diss.* II.21,6; III.17,24; III.22,67-76; IV.1,4.

[42]Braun, Gesammelte Studien, 161.

[43]Ibid., 166.

[44]"San Paolo (1 Cor. 7, 29b-31a) e Diogene il Cinico," *Biblica* 58/2 (1977): 237-45.

[45]The emphasis on ἀγάπη and the tendency to ethicize the ὡς μή exhortations are without exegetical grounds.

completely "at home" in Paul is certainly correct. It points to the apparent inconsistency in Paul's teachings with respect to the importance of sharing experiences with others, getting involved with others, sharing the joys and sorrows of others, in other passages (compare Romans 12:9-10; 13-15; even 1 Corinthians 7:12; 9:19-20; 14:13-14), and the counsel in the passage before us apparently in favor of detachment.

At any rate, his observation serves to emphasize the importance of clarifying the origin and function of the passage. However strange Braun and others think the inclusion of the passage in 1 Corinthians 7, they nevertheless take it to be of Pauline origin—by way of Stoic influence. For Braun, the passage, in spite of its strange sentiment as far as Pauline teaching goes, is still reflective of a "stoa-nahe Position."

I disagree. The point of similarity between Epictetus and Paul is the detachment that is counseled. But, as pointed out above, in the discussion concerning "Gnostic" morality and detachment from the world,[46] the detachment need not be based on one common set of motives, or even emerge from one community or worldview. The detachment that comes to expression in 1 Corinthians 7:29b-31a does not represent simply a Pauline aberration from pure Stoic doctrine; it is basically non-Stoic is motivation, if we take seriously the function of verse 29a as the ground for the exhortations.[47] The Stoics did not ground their ethical teachings on the conviction of the imminence of the End of the world. They concerned themselves with the pursuit of εὐδαιμονία as the summum bonum. Concern with eschatology was not primary, although it was thought that human actions and relationships should be influenced by the knowledge of human mortality.[48]

Penna is surely correct in being cautious in drawing conclusions about influence on account of formal parallelism between Diogenes Laertius's citation and the passage under review. Penna's retreat back into Stoicism

---

[46]Pp. 35-37.

[47]We have already suggested that v. 31b must be viewed with suspicion as an original part of vv. 29-31, on account of the emphasis it places upon the transience of the things of the world, as opposed to the shortness of the time remaining before the end. See above, pp. 33-35.

[48]See J. N. Sevenster, *Paul and Seneca*, NovTest Suppl. 4 (Leiden: E. J. Brill, 1961) 231; and Bruno Bauer, *Christus und die Caesaren: Der Ursprung des Christentums aus dem roemischen Griechentum* (Hildescheim: Olms, 1877; rpr. 1879) 47, for discussion about parallels.

as a general mediating background leaves us where Braun picks up the matter and the problems inherent in his argument.

Eschatological Prophecy

By far, most interpreters either argue for[49] or assume[50] eschatological prophecy as the provenance of verses 29-31.

The imminence motif comes to expression in 1 Corinthians 7:29-31 in two statements: ὁ καιρὸς συνεσταλμένος ἐστιν (v. 29a); παράγει γὰρ τὸ σχῆμα τοῦ κόσμου τούτου (v. 31b). In the first statement ὁ καιρός refers to the period before the End. Συνεσταλμένος affirms the imminence of the End, the passive form indicative of the theocentric perspective of apocalyptic. Parallel to verse 29a as the ground of the ὡς μή exhortations is the second statement (v. 31b). Παράγει occurs only in this context in Paul. The present tense points to the motivation behind the exhortations as related to a view of the nature of the present order. This *suggests* an origin different from verses 29-31a.

Again, both affirmations have parallels in the eschatological prophecies of both Judaism and early Christianity. What is not clear is the nature of the relationship, not so much between the eschatological affirmations and the exhortations (this relationship has already been determined[51]), as between the affirmations themselves. That is, we must determine how the ὡς μή exhortations in our passage should be understood against the two eschatological affirmations that bracket them.

---

[49]Müller, *Prophetie und Predigt im NT;* Darrell Doughty, "Heiligkeit und Freiheit: Eine exegetische Untersuchung der Anwendung des paulinischen Freiheitsgedankens in 1 Kor. 7" (diss., Göttingen, 1965); Wolfgang Schrage, "Die Stellung zur Welt bei Paulus, Epiket und in der Apokayptik," *ZThK* 61 (1964); Weiss, *Der erste Korintherbrief;* Jörg Baumgarten, *Paulus und die Apokalyptik,* WMANT 44 (Neukirchen: Neukirchen Verlag, 1979).

[50]John Gager, "Functional Diversity in Paul's Use of End-Time Language," *JBL* 89 (1970); Franzjosef Frotzheim, *Christologie und Eschatologie bei Paulus,* Forschung zur Bibel 35 (Gesamtherstellung: Echter Verlag, 1979); Hans-Heinrich Schade, *Apokalyptische Christologie bei Paulus,* Göttinger Theologische Arbeiten 18 (Göttingen: Vandenhoeck & Ruprecht, 1981); Franz Laub, *Eschatologische Verkuendigung und Lebensgestaltung nach Paulus,* Biblische Untersuchungen Herausgegeben von Otto Kuss 10 (Regensburg: Verlag Friedrich Pustet, 1973); Gottfried Hierzenberger, *Weltbewertung bei Paulus nach 1 Kor. 7, 29-31* (Düsseldorf: Patmos-Verlag, 1967); Werner Wolbert, *Ethische Argumentation und paraenese in 1 Kor. 7* (Düsseldorf: Patmos-Verlag, 1981).

[51]Cf. the discussion above regarding γάρ and τὸ λοιπόν as signals for determining the nature of the relationship between the affirmations and exhortations.

As mentioned earlier, most interpreters of our passage assume or accept the influence of either Jewish or early Christian eschatological prophecy on verses 29a and 31b. These interpreters can be divided into two categories—(1) those who see the passage against the background of Jewish/early Christian prophecy concerning the End, but see the meaning of the ὡς μή exhortations against another, different horizon; and (2) those who see the entire passage against the background of prophecy concerning the end time. Darrell Doughty and Wolfgang Schrage, respectively, have been the most vigorous discussants of the questions associated with categories (1) and (2).

Critique

1. Schrage's approach is exegetically sound. It represents respect for the clear linkage in the passage between the eschatological statements and the ὡς μή exhortations. It reflects understanding of the importance of both τὸ λοιπόν (v. 29b) and γάρ (v. 31b) in the linkage between the formal elements of the passage.[52] Doughty, on the other hand, although recognizing the presence of the links,[53] continues to interpret the passage as though the links had little importance. He proceeds to interpret the eschatological language as that which betrays the "understanding of Christian existence,"[54] and the ὡς μή exhortations as the model of existence in the world.[55] The problem here, of course, is that the clear linkage between the eschatological statements and the exhortations is ignored. There is little evidence to support the argument that the eschatological statement in verse 29a points to anything other than the conviction that the end time is near. It cannot be established that the issue here has to do simply with an understanding of the "time" (καιρός) in which the Christian community already exists as the time which is already determined by God's eschatological intervention (συνεσταλμένος).[56] It is surely overinterpretation to suggest that κόσμος, in verse 31b, "refers to the historical possibilities for man's worldly existence, in relation to which man wins or loses his

---

[52]"Die Stellung zur Welt bei Paulus," 137.

[53]"Heiligkeit und Freiheit," 206, citing Schrage.

[54]"The Presence and Future of Salvation in Corinth," 69.

[55]Ibid., 70-72.

[56]Ibid., 69.

life.''[57] Doughty seems prematurely to have imported ideas from other spheres of thought to explain the passage. Verse 29a does not support an understanding of the ὡς μή exhortations based on anything other than the affirmation of the imminence of the end. So verse 29a was left unaccounted for by Doughty, as it was collapsed into verse 31b(—35).

2. Verse 31b has been the cause of considerable problems in the interpretation of our passage. Because the verse includes the present tense verb παράγει, Schrage is forced to confess a difference here from apocalyptic texts, especially 6 Ezra 16:40-44. But this does not lead him to conclude that the entire passage is either antiapocalyptic or nonapocalyptic. He concludes only that Paul's eschatology is not simply future-oriented.[58]

But that Schrage could not explain the presence of verse 31b is clear. No matter how much emphasis is placed on Paul's eschatology as other than simply future-oriented, it is clear that verse 31b does not fit well in *verses 29-31*, or in Schrage's arguments. Verse 29a, without doubt, reflects a situation in which the expectation of the end is of cardinal importance. Verse 31b reflects a situation in which the End may still be of importance, but of more importance is the nature of the present social order. I would suggest, again, that this is one strong argument in favor of the proposal that verse 31b has an origin different from that of verses 29b-31a.

Doughty, because he thinks it important to continue with his thesis concerning the meaning of the exhortations and the function of the eschatological statements, argues that verse 31b is an extrapolation of verse 29a. Ironically, it is because of his penchant for existentialist overinterpretation of the passage that Doughty is able to see the correct horizon and importance of verse 31b. He attempts to harmonize both eschatological statements and opts for verse 31b as the key to the interpretation of them both. This forced a strained interpretation (that is, underplaying) of verse 29a, while it allowed a clarifying interpretation of verse 31b.[59]

3. As for the interpretation of ὡς μή itself Schrage accepts eschatological dualism in the background: the time is short, a tension is created between future and present. The ὡς μή exhortations encourage limited engagement in this world for no reason other than because this world's

---

[57]Ibid.

[58]"Die Stellung zur Welt bei Paulus," 148.

[59]"The Presence and Future of Salvation in Corinth," 69-70.

course is running out.[60] One can continue to buy, sell, and marry, in sum, to use this world. But because the things of the world are short-lived one should not involve oneself in the things of the world to a degree that would cause one to lose sight of this conviction.[61]

Although he rightly ties the ὡς μή directly to the affirmation about the imminence of the end, Schrage does often seem to be tempted by the idea that ὡς μή could have to do with a certain ethical posture in the world. He confesses that it is difficult to come to grips with the meaning of the exhortations until the fourth example, in which the participles on both sides of the ὡς μή are not the same for the first time (v. 30).[62] Here it could be supposed that the ὡς μή could mean that one is to buy ὡς μή, not only because the things purchased will not always be, but also because the grasping of these things is not good.[63] Schrage most clearly mirrors the interpreter's dilemma when he tries to explain that what is meant by the marriage example (reading the latter examples back into it) is not renunciation of the sexual life ("Verzicht auf den Geschlechtsverkehr"), but a different attitude (supposedly from that of the world?).[64] Here he has fallen into the ethicizing/spiritualizing trap created by his harmonizing of verses 29a and 31b, albeit with 29, not 31b, as the key verse. The emphasis in the latter on the present has influenced an ethicization of the exhortations.

Doughty, of course, could hardly have failed to fall into the ethicizing trap. Given the attempt to harmonize not only the two eschatological statements, but the entire passage with the verses that follow (32-35), given also the rather subtle (only insofar as it is not named) existentialist interpretation, it is little wonder that the exhortations are understood as a type of ethical teaching. That the ὡς μή exhortations cannot simply mean what Schrage and Doughty argue is clear from the linkages with the eschatological affirmations. The exhortations encourage limited engagement in the world because of the conviction that the time remaining before the End is short. Ethical posture or discrimination is not the *primary* consideration. To be

---

[60]"Die Stellung zur Welt bei Paulus," 149-52.

[61]Ibid., 151.

[62]Ibid.; see the discussion on p. 29 above.

[63]Ibid.

[64]Ibid.

married, to weep, to rejoice, to buy and sell, to use the world ὡς μή is to
use it in a manner not specified for every circumstance, but in a manner,
we are meant to understand, that would allow one readiness for the End.
The world may be engaged, but not seriously, not with a sense of ulti-
macy.

Both Doughty and Schrage correctly recognize the significance of verse
31b as the key verse that ties the ὡς μή exhortations to the larger context
of discussion in which the subject of concern is the believers' orientation
to the world. Such concern is broached in language suggestive of the perennial duration of the relevant factors. But verse 29a proves an embar-
rassment. Granted, the emphasis in verses 29a and 31b could be combined
in eschatological prophecies. But why would they be *formally* separated
as in our passage? What should be made of the apparent freestanding quality of each proclamation relative to the other and to the exhortations?

It is unsatisfactory to posit verse 31b (+ 32-35) as the base for the exhortations without accounting for the first proclamation in 29a (so
Doughty). It is equally unsatisfactory to argue that verse 29a functions as
the base for the exhortations without clarifying the logic or function of the
second proclamation in 31b and the extrapolation in 32-35 (so Schrage).

These and other questions force again the question of the provenance
of the exhortations in verses 29b-31a.

The Non-Pauline Origin of Verses 29b-31a

It is precisely because the immediate interpretation of the passage—
verses 32-35—leans away from the obvious linkage of the exhortations with
the eschatological affirmation in verse 29a that the question of the non-
Pauline origin of the passage is forced upon us.

Schrage hints at this origin when he suggests that the passage is "ein
apokalyptisches Traditionsstück."[65] Schrage suggests this because, otherwise, the chapter would appear to betray great inconsistencies in Paul.[66]
On this Schrage does not elaborate.

Although there may be no *one* convincing argument, there are a number of arguments that, when taken together, lead us to conclude that verses
29b-31a are of *non-Pauline origin:* (1) the introductory formula—τοῦτο

---

[65]"Die Stellung zur Welt bei Paulus," 139, 153.

[66]Ibid., 139.

δέ φημι (v. 29)—as already stated, occurs elsewhere only in 1 Corinthians 15:50 and there introduces a *pre-Pauline* logion; (2) vv. 29-31 interrupts the discussion in 25-40; and (3) συστέλλω, τὸ λοιπόν + ἵνα, ἀγοραζεῖν, χρῆσθαι + κόσμος are words and phrases rarely or singularly used by Paul.[67]

Siegfried Schulz understands our passage as the *locus classicus* for an expression of the understanding of the relationship to the world in early Christian apocalypticism, or at least that branch of it which accepted the Gentile mission, and rejected the Mosaic Law as rule for the community.[68] This community, to which Paul belonged, did not base its practice and preaching of distance to the world on a tradition of (spirit/matter) dualism. The "Gnostic" worldview was not embraced. Stoicism has certain parallels, but the differences are more pronounced.[69]

According to Schulz, we are much closer to the community from which our passage comes if we turn to late Jewish and Jewish-Christian apocalypticism and the basic tension between the two ages which is to be found there. What develops from this tension, from the expectation of the future age and the establishment of the reign of God, are two reactions: (1) passive waiting, or endurance; and (2) an active exodus from society.[70] The community from which our passage comes accepted neither of the responses *in toto,* but seems to have opted for a type of *inner-worldly* distance from the things of the world.[71]

This inner-worldly detachment was not *merely* moral or ethical in motivation and form. It was first a delimitation from the world based on an *eschatological* dualism, "taking rise from the expectation that he who now flees the world will have his renunciation richly compensated by future heavenly goods."[72] The detachment had as its motive a concern about

---

[67]Siegfried Schulz, "Evangelium und Welt, Hauptprobleme einer Ethik des Neuen Testaments," *Neues Testament und Christliche Existenz,* Festschrift für Herbert Braun, H. D. Betz and Luise Schottroff, eds. (Tübingen: Mohr, 1973) 483-501.

[68]Ibid., 486.

[69]Ibid., 487.

[70]Ibid. Qumran is in mind here.

[71]Schulz, "Evangelium und Welt," 488; cf. also 2 Bar. 44:8; 10:9, 13: (1) En. 48:7.

[72]Rudolf Bultmann, *Theology of the New Testament,* Kendrick Grobel, trans., 2 vols (New York: Scribners, 1951-1955) 1:100.

readiness for the End, thought to be imminent. Thus, all worldly concerns are *relativized* in importance. Only secondarily is the concern about the ethical and moral inferiority of the world.

Our closest parallel is the 6 Ezra (2 Esdras) passage, to which we have already made reference. If our argument that verse 31b was not an original part of verses 29-31a is valid, 6 Ezra 16:35-44 parallels our passage both formally and in terms of content. As in 6 Ezra there is the proclamation regarding the imminence of calamities, so in our passage there is proclamation regarding the shortness of the time remaining before the End. Just as in 6 Ezra there are exhortations to the readers concerning the response to the situation, so in our passage exhortations follow. In 6 Ezra the readers are exhorted to respond to the world as though in battle. They are not encouraged to leave the world, but "in the midst of" the world, so "be like strangers" (v. 40). They are exhorted to relativize the importance of all things worldly in light of the imminence of the calamities ahead. Not to relativize the importance of all things worldly is to render oneself unable to escape at the time of plunder. Not to loosen oneself from the world is to be unprepared to flee. Not to sit loose from the things of the world is to find oneself engrossed and distracted and eventually vulnerable to attack.[73]

Mainly because the situation to which 6 Ezra 16 speaks is one of consciousness of impending doom for a particular set of sins and transgressions, I do not think that the author was here influenced by Paul. But 6 Ezra and our passage would seem to be part of a tradition in which apocalyptic consciousness or spirituality called for detachment from the world in the form of a relativizing of the importance of all things worldly. As mentioned above, this tradition was a prophetic tradition that encouraged a particular response to the conviction of the imminence of calamities.[74]

Paul makes use of this type of traditional prophetic utterance in 1 Corinthians 7 in order to encourage the Corinthians toward a certain type of response to the world. It need not be argued that Paul here quotes *verbatim* from any written or oral prophecy; it is enough to argue here that he makes use of a fixed or stereotyped *pattern* of eschatological prophecy to meet the immediate needs of his argument.

---

[73]Cf. esp. 6 Ezra (2 Esdras) 16:45-48.

[74]See above, pp. 24-25.

The Function of Verses 29b-31a

Paul makes use of the eschatological prophecy in 1 Corinthians 7 in order to counter the understanding and model of Christian existence that he extrapolates from the Corinthians' questions. He wants to convince the Corinthians that Christian existence is to be experienced in the world, but not on the world's terms. Some distance is appropriate, but this distance need not be spatial. Following the argument, which we have discovered as a thread throughout the chapter, Paul, with the use of the traditional eschatological prophecy, continues to advise the Corinthians against equating Christian existence with worldly status, or, more accurately, the loss of worldly status. The prophecy serves to offer a model of existence *in* the world without granting any importance to the world. This results in a compromise of sorts, since some of the Corinthians were totally rejecting the world. It also represents a *nonelitist* model of Christian existence: no particular χάρισμα is required. No special category or class of persons is called for to meet the standards. Both the "weak" and the "strong" can "be . . . have . . . as if not."

Given the different emphasis that is struck in verse 31b as far as proclamation grounding the exhortations is concerned, and, given the verses that follow (32-35) as reinterpretation of the meaning of the exhortations in the context of 1 Corinthians 7, it is clear that the *eschatological* character of the prophecy was not the reason for its inclusion in 1 Corinthians 7. Important to to Paul was the type of *response to the world* that comes to expression in the exhortations. The relativizing of all things worldly fits squarely with his argument throughout the chapter that worldly statuses or conditions are a thing ἀδιάφορον with respect to status with God.

With verse 31b—if not already with τὸ λοιπόν in 29—Paul betrays his real concern. Although Paul continues to believe in the imminence of the End, in 1 Corinthians 7 he is less so concerned. Verses 31b-35 show his interest to be other than that of countering "realized eschatology," thought by most exegetes to have been an index of dogma for some of the Corinthians.[75] Paul himself *de-eschatologizes:* in 31b, he emphasizes, instead of the imminence of the End, the transience of the things of the world. Verses 32-35 continues this emphasis by addressing the issue of the ramification of engaging, even to a limited degree, the things of the world. In this discussion the goal behind the relativizing of the world is set forth. Thus, verses 32-35 require the same detailed analysis as the preceding section.

---

[75]Cf. Doughty, "Presence," 62-66.

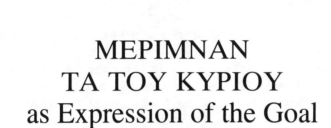

Chapter 3

MEPIMNAN
TA TOY KYPIOY
as Expression of the Goal
of a Model
# of Ascetic Behavior
(1 Corinthians 7:32-35)

ἈΜΕΡΙΜΝΟΣ

With the first person singular θέλω,[1] the conjunctive particle δέ,[2] ὑμᾶς as the sign of change of addressees,[3] and ἀμερίμνους as the sign of a shift both in type of language and emphasis of discussion, verse 32 represents the beginning of a significant turn in Paul's response to the Corinthians in

---

[1]This is in order to resume the person and form of address cut by vv. 29-31. N.B.: ἐγώ, ὑμῶν in v. 28; θέλω, ὑμᾶς in v. 32. The first person in v. 29a (φημί) should be discounted, since it is governed by an introductory prophetic formula (τοῦτο δέ φημι) rather than by the personal form of address in evidence throughout chapter (vv. 25, 26, 28, 40).

[2]Here used to mark transition, with some adversative force. The contrast would be between the worldview that the eschatological prophecy in vv. 29-31a brings to expression and that understanding of "world" that is to be explained in vv. 32-35.

[3]See n. 1 above. There is no second-person address in vv. 29-31a.

1 Corinthians 7.[4] Verse 31b serves not only to help establish verses 29-31a as eschatological prophecy employed by Paul to serve his purposes in the context of 1 Corinthians 7,[5] it also provides the transition to Paul's *reinterpretation and application* of that prophecy in verses 32-35. As it emphasizes the transient nature of "this world" (τὸ σχῆμα τοῦ κόσμου τούτου), verse 31b serves as an introduction to verses 32-35, which has to do with the relevance of "this world" (ὁ κόσμος οὗτος) for believers.

With verses 32-35 an attempt is made to explain how the ὡς μή exhortations should be interpreted and applied through modification (that is, a relativizing) of the importance of the imminent expectation: there is a shift away from the imminence motif (v. 29a) as ground for the exhortations to another ground—ἀμέριμνος and μεριμνᾷ τὰ τοῦ κυρίου (vv. 32, 34.)

With ἀμερίμνους, the Pauline reinterpretation first comes into focus. Cognates (μέριμνα) appear in verses 32b, 33, and 34; synonyms (σύμφορον, εὔσχημον, εὐπάρεδρον, ἀπερισπάστως) in verse 35b.[6] Among the Greeks ἀμέριμνος, like the term ἀπάθεια among the Stoic philosophers, was used generally to express indifference, lack of concern.[7] In the piety of the LXX[8] and in early Christianity[9] the term began to take on religious significance. That the term is used in a religious sense in

---

[4]We would have expected some elaboration of the imminence motif first struck in v. 26, but v. 32 takes a different turn in the discussion—regarding μεριμνᾶν, "care."

[5]Cf. ch. 2 above for a discussion of the origin and function of 7:29b-31a. I have sought to demonstrate that the exhortations were originally part of eschatological prophecy—prophecy regarding the imminence of the end time and the type of response to the world that should be made in light of this conviction.

[6]Ἀπερισπάστως also serves, with ἀμερίμνους, v. 32, as an *inclusio*. Cf. Helen North's discussion of the language of moral and ethical teaching among the Greek and Roman philosophers, in *Sōphrosynē* (Ithaca: Cornell University Press, 1966). Although North does not discuss these terms, it is clear from her discussion of the various uses of σωφροσύνη and its synonyms that μεριμνᾶν and synonyms in 1 Cor. 7 served much the same purposes—as expressions of the ideal Greek virtues of temperance and moderation. As for ἀπερισπαστᾶν in particular, Weiss, *Der erste Korintherbrief*, 205n.2, first noted the frequency of its occurrence in the late Stoa.

[7]Sophocles, *Ai.*, 1207; Sextus Emp., *Adv. Eth.*, 117; see R. Bultmann, ἀμέριμνος, *TDNT* 4:593 for discussion.

[8]Cf. Pss. 35(36):8; 61(62):9; 90(91):4; 107(108):10; Jer 49:11; Isa. 32:18; also 4 Macc.

1 Corinthians 7:32 is made clear by the larger context. Verse 32 in itself is meant to serve as clarification of the ὡς μή exhortations. Paul means for the latter to be understood as exhortations to a life ἀμέριμνος. The precise meaning of the term here is not yet made clear: we cannot be sure at this point whether Paul desires that the Corinthians be indifferent, namely, without any care whatsoever, or whether he is here only counseling a particular type of concern, using the term equivocally or, perhaps, tongue in cheek.

Μεριμνᾶν is found in Greek from the time of Hesiod. It had a range of meanings from "to care" (for someone, something)[10] to "ambition" and "anxiety."[11] The term does not occur either among the philosophers or in Hellenistic Judaism.[12] It does occur in the LXX, usually denoting a striving after, or anxiety of some type.[13]

In early Christian literature μεριμνᾶν usually has a negative sense— "striving after something," "anxious about something."[14] But in the passage in 1 Corinthians μεριμνᾶν must have a *neutral* meaning, since it has objects that serve to qualify it, and that in a starkly, even dualistically contrasting manner.[15] It is taken for granted that μεριμνᾶν is a universally human disposition: it is neither good nor bad in itself. As far as Paul is concerned, μεριμνᾶν becomes negative when its object is the world, positive when it is the Lord. When the object of the μεριμνᾶν is the world, division of purpose and commitment occur (μεμέρισται).

8:26 (ἀταραξία); in (Book of) Wisdom, in connection with the pursuit and possession of wisdom: 6:15, 7:23.

[9]The term occurs elsewhere in the New Testament only in Matt. 28:14; there without religious connotations. Also cf. Hermas *Mand.* 5.2.3; Ignatius *Poly* 7:1.

[10]Cf. Soph., *Oed. Tyr.*, 1460; 1124.

[11]Cf. Aesch., *Eum.* 132; Pindar, *Olymp.* 1, 109:2, 60; *Nem*, 3, 69; Xenophon, *Cyrop.* VIII, 7, 112. Also often linked with φόβος, Aesch., *Sept. c Theb*, 287ff. In Plato, *Cri.*, 44c8; *Rep.* I 344e.16; VIII 563d.8; *Crat.*, 414d.1; *Laws* XI 917a2; *Apol.*, 2932; *Symp.*, 220c.7; *Pol.*, 287a.5; *Euphr.*, 3c5.

[12]Instead, we find, according to Bultmann (*TDNT* 4:590), φροντίς, φροντίζειν.

[13]Ps. 54:22; Prov. 27:12; Sir. 30:24; 38:29; 42:9; Esth. 1:1; Wis. 12:22; 2 Macc. 6:10.

[14]Cf. Matt. 6:31; 10:19; 1 Pet. 5:7; Phil. 4:6; Luke 21:34; Herm., *Vis.*, 4.2.5.

[15]Contra Jerome, Murphy-O'Connor, *1 Corinthians*, New Testament Message 10 (Wilmington DE: Michael Glazier, Inc., 1979; rpr. ed., 1982) 74-75.

A dualism of sorts is established in the passage, signaled by the two
sets of antithetical *stichoi,* structurally divided between the sexes:[16]

ὁ ἄγαμος μεριμνᾷ τὰ τοῦ κυρίου, πῶς ἀρέσῃ τῷ κυρίῳ
ὁ δὲ γαμήσας μεριμνᾷ τὰ τοῦ κόσμου, πῶς ἀρέσῃ τῇ γυναικί
. . .
ἡ γυνὴ ἡ ἄγαμος καὶ ἡ παρθένος μεριμνᾷ τὰ τοῦ κυρίου . . .
ἡ δὲ γαμήσασα μεριμνᾷ τὰ τοῦ κόσμου πῶς ἀρέσῃ τῷ ἀνδρί

The polarity or dualism lies not in the division of the sets of *stichoi* along the
lines of gender, nor ultimately in one's situation vis-à-vis marriage. The polarity lies in the *object* of μεριμνᾶν. There are only two such possible objects—the world (τὰ τοῦ κόσμου), or the Lord (τὰ τοῦ κυρίου).
Μεριμνᾶν itself is not inveighed against; it is after all through μεριμνᾶν
that one can be ἀρέσῃ τῷ κυρίῳ (v. 32) or ἁγία καὶ τῷ σώματι καὶ
τῷ πνεύματι (v. 34). The goal is to become completely devoted to the Lord
(v. 35).

The ὡς μή exhortations, then, are translated by Paul into that state of
affairs in which one is not divided in loyalty or devotion to the Lord. This
means that one who has a wife, to take the most relevant example for the
Corinthians, is exhorted to relate to his wife in such a way that devotion
to the Lord does not suffer. Already it has been said by Paul that one already married need not desert one's wife in the interest of devotion to the
Lord (v. 27; also v. 12-13). One need not separate from wife *or husband,*
business, or the cultivation of friendship, in order to be pleasing to the Lord.
One can remain in the state or condition in which one was called into faith,
since all that is relevant with respect to faith is τήρησις ἐντολῶν θεοῦ
("keeping the commandments of God," v. 19), that is, as exemplified in
Christ (cf. Rom. 2:25; Gal. 5:6, 14-15).

In light of the entire thrust of his advice in 1 Corinthians 7, we must
understand Paul's reference to the married and unmarried man (vv. 32, 33),
and to the married and unmarried woman (v. 34), as somewhat rhetorical.
That is, it is unlikely that we are meant to understand by these references
any attempt to exhaust his understanding of or teaching regarding marriage. We are meant to understand the references as attempts to describe
typical "worldly" situations in which all—including believers—find
themselves. Everyone is associated in some way with others, and these as-

---

[16]See Weiss, *Der erste Korintherbrief,* 201, 202-203, for a discussion of text-critical
problems; also Conzelmann, *1 Corinthians,* 134; Robertson and Plummer, ICC, 157.

sociations involve emotional ties and responsibilities, concern, care—
μεριμνᾶν. Marriage is just *one* example of such associations. It requires
care for the spouse. This is not in itself negative; it is an observation. Neither married life nor care is inveighed against in any absolute sense. Married life is here simply lifted up both as an example of typical "worldly"
involvement and as a response to the Corinthians' particular questions.

We are, nevertheless, still left without clarity with respect eto the
meaning of the polarity established between the objects of μεριμνᾶν. How
did Paul want his readers to understand and apply the counsel to "remain," since he argues that Christian existence does not require any particular "worldly" status or condition? The whole chapter, it must be
confessed, betrays little enthusiasm on the part of Paul for the married state.
He offers counsel that discourages a universal change for Christians from
the married state to the single celibate state for the sake of holiness (vv.
12-24), but that also encourages a type of detachment in the context of the
married state in order to pursue "the things of the Lord" without distraction (vv. 32-35). We are left to conclude that Paul is saying that *some* type
of renunciation *within* the parameters of the relationship of marriage, or
any other "worldly" relationship or involvement, is required for holiness.
This is the meaning and importance of the ὡς μή exhortations. *They represent a model of "asceticism" Paul thinks necessary and appropriate for
those whose goal it is to please the Lord.*

Perhaps due to the delicate and novel situation in Corinth which
prompted the questions regarding marriage and celibacy in the first place,
Paul presents his views in an awkward manner. He draws upon and jux-
taposes not only different languages, but different worldviews, in his response to the questions. Whatever the reason, later readers and interpreters,
if not also the initial readers and interpreters, have been left unable to determine with any degree of certainty the actual type of response here counseled.[17] We can be certain only of the *goal* of the response or model of
"asceticism," and of the rejection of other "models," namely, the options for either changing stations in life (renouncing relationships with others), or remaining in one's station in life with all of the features typically
associated with that station (for example, the μεριμνᾶν about which Paul
speaks in vv. 33 and 34). What is clear is the importance of being ἀμέρ-

---

[17]See the history of interpretation discussion in Hurd, *The Origin of 1 Corinthians,*
ch. 1.

ιμνος, but only that one might be capable of directing full attention to "the things of the Lord." But it is not clear how ἀμέριμνος was to be understood. How was it meant to be applied?

Parallels

Discussion of possible parallels in social orientation is warranted in order to help at least narrow the range of possibilities against which to interpret the counsel Paul attempts to offer.

First Corinthians 7:5 and Jewish Piety

First Corinthians 7:5 is an appropriate starting point, since here Paul implies that marriage can be distracting of the prayer life.[18] That there be no such distraction on a permanent basis, abstinence from sexual activity is "conceded" (συγγνώμην) , but only for a short while (πρὸς καιρόν). Commentators see in the background of this advice the Jewish tradition of temporary abstinence for the sake of a vow, the study of the Torah, or prayer.[19] Two important points must be made regarding the practice as Paul seems to see it in 7:5: first, it would be occasional, occurring only in exceptional circumstances;[20] second, it would, at any rate, always be temporary,[21] never an ongoing permanent pattern of behavior.

The advice given in verses 32-35, however, does not concern the exceptional circumstance or the temporary; it has to do with a *permanent* model of existence. The two sets of counsel—7:5, 32-35—*are* similar in

---

[18] ἵνα σχολάσητε τῇ προσευχῇ.

[19]Robertson and Plummer, ICC, 134; Weiss, Der erste Korintherbrief, 174; Conzelmann, *1 Corinthians,* 117; Hans Leitzmann, *Eschatologie, Verkündigung, und Lebengestaltung nach Paulus: Eine Untersuchung zum Wirken des Apostels beim Aufbau der Gemeinde in Thessalonike,* Biblische Untersuchungen Herausgegeben von Otto Kuss 10 (Regensburg: Verlag Friedrich Pustet, 1973) 30. Temporary abstention for spiritual purpose is advised: Eccles. 3.5; Joel 2:16; Zech. 12:12-14. Cf. esp. T. Naph. 8: Καιρὸς γὰρ συνουσίας γυναικὸς καὶ καιρὸς ἐγκρατείας εἰς προσευχὴν αὐτοῦ. Also cf. George W. E. Nickelsburg and Michael E. Stone, eds., *Faith and Piety in Early Judaism: Texts and Documents* (Philadelphia: Fortress Press, 1983) 109.

[20]Robertson and Plummer, ICC, 134; εἰ μήτι ἄν suggests the tentativeness of the advice.

[21]Cf. Hermann L. Strack and Paul Billerbeck, *Kommentar zum Neuen Testament aus Talmud und Midrash* (München: Beck, 1922-1961) 3:371-72 for such vows. The aim is always study or prayer. Cf. also 1 Thess. 2:17 over against 2 Cor. 7:8; Gal. 2:5; Phlm. 15.

that the motivation seems to be to realize a state of existence in which one will not be distracted from higher concerns (however defined). But it is unlikely that either the Jewish custom of practicing temporary abstinence, or—if it does not belong to this tradition—1 Corinthians 7:5, is behind Paul's counsel in verses 32-35. In the latter, not only does Paul go beyond the advocacy of the temporary, he commends the permanent behavior with enthusiasm, and without equivocation and qualification.

With respect to marriage itself, it must be said that, on the whole, Judaism revered it.[22] Family life was deemed important and praiseworthy— even for priests.[23] In the rabbinic literature a man is bidden to marry and have children.[24] Neither the Rechabites nor the Nazarites proscribed marriage, and the report on the Essenes seems contradictory. The celibate Therapeutae, unlike the Essenes, did admit women into the community, but neither community, including Paul's Pharisaic party, had significant influence in Judaism with respect to establishing or spreading asceticism of any type.[25] It is unlikely that Paul's advice in verses 32-35 was bequeathed to him by any denomination of Judaism without considerable translation, or non-Jewish influence.

Non-Jewish Cultic Asceticism

No scholar, to my knowledge, sees any type of cultic asceticism as the background of the counsel that Paul gives in 1 Corinthians 7:32-35.

Cultic abstinence of some type has been identified in almost every culture in antiquity, as well as in more contemporary "primitive" cultures.[26]

---

[22]Bernhard Lohse, *Askese und Mönchtum in der Antike und in der alten Kirche* (München u. Wien: R. Oldenburg, 1969) 79-113; Kurt Niederwimmer, *Askese und Mysterium: Über Ehe, Ehescheidung und Eheverzicht in den Anfängen des christlichen Glaubens* (Göttingen: Vanderhoeck & Ruprecht, 1975) 13-41.

[23]Cf. Genesis 1:28-29; Enslin, *The Ethics of Paul,* 181. There was a tradition of proscription against marriage for priests in some cultures. This will be discussed further, below.

[24]"He who lives without a wife lives without joy and blessing, without protection and peace," *Yebamot* 62a; cf. also 63ab; *Mekilta, Yitro* 8; *Shabbat* 31a. *Yabamot* 63a: "A single man is not a complete man." Cf. Strack-Billerbeck, *Kommentar Zum NT,* 3.

[25]George W. E. Nickelsburg, *Jewish Literature Between the Bible and the Mishnah* (Philadelphia: Fortress Press, 1981) ch. 4; Nichelsburg and Stone, *Faith and Piety in Early Judaism,* 25-30.

[26]Mary Douglas, *Natural Symbols; Explorations in Cosmology,* 2nd ed. (London: Barrie & Jenkins, 1973); *Purity and Danger* (London: Routledge & Kegan Paul, 1966).

Concern about μίασμα in the Greek and Hellenistic cults was translated into purifications, the avoidance of certain things (for example corpses, types of animals and foods, menstruating women, childbirth, and, for priests, sexual intercourse while making sacrifices and fasting). The typical devotee of the mystery cults placed himself or herself completely at the disposal of the deity, vowing lifelong commitment. Some initiates took up residence in the temple for a probationary period of time determined by the deity. The devotee would seek ecstatic union with the deity through renunciation of the body and social intercourse. At the end of the probationary period, the devotee would return to the world.[27]

But this type of renunciation or ascetic practice is not counseled in 1 Corinthians 7. The reference to the holiness of the unmarried woman "in body and spirit" (v. 34) betrays not concern with cultic purity, but, more likely, Paul's retreat back into antiquity's generally patriarchal views regarding the purity of women, and/or his taking up of the language and sentiment of some of the Corinthians.[28]

'Απάθεια: Spiritual Detachment of the Philosophers

Andre-Jean Festugière[29] identifies two forms of religion among the Greeks of the classical age (into late antiquity): the "concrete" form, in which one communicated with one of the Olympians; the "inward" form, in which one desired to flee the world for Olympus, home of the Gods.

Festugière deems Plato largely responsible not for the origin, but for the development of the second form.[30] Plato's true philosopher is one who

---

[27]See Richard Reitzenstein, *Hellenistic Mystery Religions: Their Basic Ideas and Significance,* trans. John E. Steely (rpr.: Pittsburg: The Pickwick Press, 1978) 237-67; A. D. Nock, *Conversion: The Old and The New in Religion from Alexander The Great to Augustine of Hippo* (Oxford: Oxford University Press, 1961) 97-121; Friedrick C. Grant, ed., *Hellenistic Religions: The Age of Syncretism* (Indianapolis: Bobbs-Merrill Company, 1953) 25-32, 105-51; Ramsey MacMullen, *Paganism in the Roman Empire* (New Haven/London: Yale University Press, 1981) 42-48, 112-30. For the most recent comprehensive treatment of pollution and purification in Greek religion, cf. Parker, *Miasma: Pollution and Purification in Early Greek Religion,* esp. chs. 3, 10.

[28]See C. K. Barrett, *The First Epistle to the Corinthians,* HNTC (New York/Evanston: Harper & Row Publishers, 1968) 181. Conzelmann's comment that Paul here simply points to the whole human being misses the point regarding the singling out of the woman; cf. his *1 Corinthians,* s.v.; and especially Parker, *Miasma,* chs. 3 and 4.

[29]In his *Personal Religion among the Greeks* 2nd. ed. (Berkeley: University of California Press, 1960) ch. 3.

[30]Ibid., 37.

is driven only towards the Eternal, the supreme categories of Being. The visible world is of little importance. One must turn the soul inward upon itself in a contemplative mood. True philosophers must be detached from the world.

> From their youth up they have never known the way to the market place or law court or Council Chamber or any other place of public assembly; they never hear a decree read out or look at the text of a law. To take any interest in the revelries of political cliques, in meetings, dinner, and merry-making with flute girls, never occurs to them even in dreams. Whether any fellow citizen is well- or ill-born or has inherited some defect from his ancestors on either side, the philosopher knows no more than how many pints of water there are in the sea. He is not even aware that he knows of all this, for if he holds aloof (ἀπέχεται) it is not for reputation's sake, but because it is really only his body that sojourns in his city while his thought, disdaining (ἀτιμήσασα) all such things as worthless, takes wings, as Pindar says, "beyond the sky, beneath the earth," searching the heavens and measuring the plains, everywhere seeking the true nature of everything as a whole, never sinking to what lies close at hand.[31]

Since Plato based his entire system on the belief in the reality of the Ideas, Supreme Categories of Being, as well as the conviction that things in the visible world are but copies of the Ideas, he was forced into a dualism of sorts—the sensible, visible world over against the world of the Ideas. The visible world is characterized by constant change, or flux; the world of the Ideas is changeless.

> That which is apprehended by intelligence and reason is always in the same state, but that which is conceived by opinion with the help of sensation and without reason is always in a process of becoming and perishing and never really is.[32]

The intelligible world of the Ideas is, therefore, superior.

And the wise man will focus attention on this superior world in contemplation of the Ideas (*Symposium*, 211-12). But this can be done only when the soul of the philosopher, that part of him which is most like the world of the Ideas (*Phaedrus*, 80), is successful in escaping the prison, the

---

[31]*Theaet.*, 173de. Quotations from Plato taken from *Plato: The Collected Dialogues, Including The Letters*, Bollingen Series 71, E. Hamilton and H. Cairns, eds. (Princeton NJ: Princeton University Press, 1961). (Greek text consulted in Loeb Classical Library.)

[32]*Tim.*, 27d-28a.

living tomb, which is the body (σῶμα/σῆμα). The soul "is drawn away by the body into the realm of the variable, and loses its way and becomes confused and dizzy, as though it were fuddled" (*Phaedrus, 79c*). Only by returning unto itself and by reflecting upon itself is it able to pass over into the realm of purity, eternity, unchangeableness (*Phaedrus, 79d*).

But Plato did not teach contempt for the body or for the world. His concern was for the proper prioritizing of the things of the world, including the body. He taught that the philosopher must attach no value to the body vis-à-vis contemplation of the Ideas. It is not that the body is evil; it is that it may prove to be a hindrance to the pursuit of the things that matter most.

> So long as we keep to the body and our soul is contaminated with this imperfection, there is no chance of our ever attaining satisfactorily to our object. . . In the first place, the body provides us with innumerable distractions (μυρίας . . . ἀσχολίας) in the pursuit of our necessary substance . . . fills us with loves and desires and fears and all sorts of fancies and a great deal of nonsense, with the result that we literally never get an opportunity to think at all about anything.[33]

But the true philosopher rises above the ordinary cares and concerns of the body and the world in which the body lives, in order to give himself over completely to the pursuit of the Eternal. The body and the world are depreciated only to the extent that they distract from this pursuit. But the body itself is not mutilated. In fact, the real intent of the references to the body as prison, as distraction, is betrayed most clearly in passages such as the one below having to do with the importance of proportion and balance in human nature.

> [W]hen . . . there is an impassioned soul more powerful than the body, that soul, I say, convulses and fills with disorder the whole inner nature of man, and when eager in the pursuit of some sort of learning or study, causes wasting. . . . And once more, when a body large and too strong for the soul is united to a small and weak intelligence, then inasmuch as there are two desires natural to man—one of food for the sake of the body, and one of wisdom for the sake of the diviner part of us—then, I say, the motions of the stronger, getting the better and increasing their own power, but making the soul dull and stupid and forgetful, engender ignorance, which is the greatest of the diseases. *There is one protection against both kinds of disproportion—that we should not move the body without the soul or the*

---

[33]*Phaed.*, 66bc.

soul without the body, and thus they will be on their guard against each other and be healthy and well balanced.[34]

All the passages that encourage contemplation of the Eternal and detachment from the body and the world demand no more than "that the body be kept in its proper place, and that the philosopher attach no value to it."[35]

In Plato the desire to contemplate the Eternal was the desire "to become like god" (ὁμοίωσις θεῷ). As Festugière paraphrases Plato, it was the desire

to get the motion of one's soul in accord with the motion of the heavenly bodies, to lose oneself in the contemplation of the stars . . . to forget for an instant the frailty and the fleetingness of the things of the earth, to immerse oneself in the Eternal.[36]

This spirituality greatly influenced the Stoic philosophers of the Roman empire, especially as regards the motivation behind, and form of "retirement" from, the world.[37] Some Stoics and Epicureans shared not only Plato's priorities, but also his view of the worldly distractions with which the philosopher must deal.[38] In tracing the use of the term ἀναχωρεῖν, ἀναχώρησις in antiquity, Festugière has established the *spiritualizing* usage of the term as an index of an emphasis on inwardness among the philosophers of the Empire. Physical withdrawal (ἀναχώρησις) was deemed good, but there was thought to be something better—"withdrawal into oneself" (ἀναχωρεῖν εἰς ἑαυτόν).[39]

---

[34]*Tim.*, 88ab; emphasis mine.

[35]Joseph W. Swain, *The Hellenic Origins of Christian Asceticism* (New York: Columbia University Press, 1916) 61.

[36]Festugière, *Personal Religion among the Greeks*, 61.

[37]Ibid.; ch. 4, especially, traces use of terms among philosophers. For most of the quotations below I am indebted to Festugière.

[38]The Epicurean, Philodemus, in his treatise, Περὶ Οἰκονομίας, raised the question about what the attitude of the wise man should be regarding work (πορισμός), then provides his own answer: "But to live off the land where others farm it—that is truly in keeping with wisdom. For then one is least entangled in business (τις ὁ φιλοσοφῷ προσήκων πόρος)." Cf. Festugière, *Personal Religion among the Greeks*, 55-57. Greek text ed. C. Jensen (Leipzig, 1906).

[39]An equivalent of the terms used by the philosophers is found already in Plato, upon whom the Stoics drew for their spirituality. The passage is from the *Symposium*, 174D.

Throughout his *Epistulae Morales ad Lucilium*[40] Seneca gives counsel to retreat spiritually:

> I force my mind to concentrate, and keep it from straying to things outside itself, all outdoors may be bedlam, provided that there is no disturbance within, provided that fear is not wrangling with desire in my breast, provided that meanness and lavishness are not at odds, one harassing the other. For of what benefit is a quiet neighbourhood, if our emotions are in an uproar? . . . Real tranquility is the state reached by an unperverted mind when it is relaxed. (56.6.7)

Dio Chrysostom even wrote an entire treatise entitled Περὶ 'Αναχωρήσεως, showing thereby how significant the subject had become in philosophical circles of the day.[41]

> Just what, pray, is the meaning of the word "retirement" (ἀναχωρήσεως) and whom should we define as men who are "retiring"? Is it those who are giving up their proper tasks and activities . . . ? . . . if a man who is qualified to heal the sick, and then when the sick are friends and intimates of his, should abandon them . . . ? . . . should these men be described as "retiring"? No. . . .
> . . . clearly it is not the place where you are nor this going abroad that affords an escape from doing sundry trivial things, nor is it even one's having retired to Corinth or to Thebes, but rather the being occupied with one's own self, when one so wishes . . . the best and most profitable kind of retirement is retirement into oneself and giving attention to one's concerns, whether one happens to be in Babylon, or in Athens, or in a military camp, or alone on a little island. (*Or.* 20.1-2,7,8)

The conclusion:

> the mind should accustom itself to do and think what is essential to it everywhere, even in a perfect din as well as in perfect quiet. (*Or.* 20.26)

Socrates is on his way to dine at the home of Agathon along with Aristodemus. As they travel along together Socrates "fell into a fit of abstraction (ἑαυτῷ πως προσέχοντα τὸν νοῦν) and began to lag behind." When a slave is asked to retrieve him, it is said that he should be left alone because he often "draws apart from us wherever he may be and stands there." The lesson that the wise man, the true philosopher, can contemplate the Eternal only as he separates himself from the world, from distractions, was lost neither on Plato (who learned from Socrates) nor on later philosophers. Cf. Festugière, 58, 59.

[40]Cf. also 2.1; 25.6; 28.1.

[41]Cf. Festugière, *Personal Religion among the Greeks,* 60-61.

As emperor, Marcus Aurelius could hardly afford physical withdrawal. But he recognized that physical withdrawal alone was not important, at any rate, "since one possesses the possibility whenever one wants to use it, of retiring into oneself (εἰς ἑαυτὸν ἀναχωρεῖν). "Nowhere is there a withdrawal more calm, more free from care, than into one's own soul. . . . Therefore make this withdrawal constantly . . . be mindful of that withdrawal which you can make in the spot of earth where you now are."[42]

Philo, though positively disposed to the idea of solitude for the contemplative life,[43] nevertheless recognized the proper state of the soul as the single most important *conditio sine qua non* for contemplation:

> Many a time I have forsaken kinsfolk, friends, and home, and buried myself in the wilderness (εἰς ἐρημίαν ἐλθών) to give my attention to some subject worthy of contemplation, only to derive therefrom no profit, but to have my spirit, bitter and distraught by passion, wander to matters of a contrary kind. But then again, at other times, I have been in the midst of a great throng and have had a collected mind (ἠρεμῶ τὴν διάνοιαν). God has dispersed the crowd that besets the soul and has taught me that favorable and unfavorable conditions are not brought about by differences of place, but by God, who moves and leads the chariot of the soul in whatever way he pleases.[44]

According to Epictetus, solitude (ἐρημία) is not necessarily a good thing;[45] "one must prepare oneself for this . . . one must be able to be sufficient unto oneself and live in the company of oneself."[46] As Zeus lives alone and governs the universe, so the wise man, the philosopher, should be able to live alone, to contemplate, in order to help remedy the ills of society.[47]

---

[42]*Meditations* 4.3.2-3 (trans. Festugière).

[43]Philo does not use the term ἀναχωρεῖν in the spiritual sense as seen in the other philosophers. But many words derived from μόνος (e.g., μοναρχεία, μοναστήριον) are used. His description ("romantic") of the Essenes and Therapeutae betrays his interest in and support of physical withdrawal. Cf. *De Vita Contemplativa*.

[44]*Leg. All.* 2.85 (trans. Festugière); cf. also *Spec. Leg.* 2.20-21; 4.88: *Mut. Nom.*, 32; *Fuga*, 38, 63; *Opif. Mund.*, 144, 151.

[45]*Diss.* 3.13; 4.4; life in the desert (ἐρημία) never seems to Epictetus an ideal. See Festugière, *Personal Religion among the Greeks*, 63 n. 24.

[46]*Diss.* 3.13, 7-8.

[47]Festugière, *Personal Religion among the Greeks*, 64; cf. *Diss.* 3.13.8.

Plotinus is reported to have had a love for withdrawal, often taking refuge in the estate of a friend.[48] So serious was he about it that he asked permission of the emperor Gallienus to restore for his use a small town in Campania as a kind of retreat for the training of pupils and engagement with other philosophers. The project did not come to reality, but it helps us to see how important was the idea of withdrawal for Plotinus and others.[49]

In spite of his inclination toward physical retirement, Plotinus did recognize the importance of spiritual retreat: "there is another life of soul, and other activities, and that which is punished is different. The ascent (ἀναχώρησις) and separation (χωρισμός) is not only from this body but from all that has been added."[50]

> Thus must we flee from this world and separate ourselves from all that has been added to us; thus must we cease to be this composite thing, this animate body, slave to the corporeal nature which has barely preserved a trace of the soul; all that depends on this life is corporeal. It is to that other soul, the soul that comes from without, that is movement toward beauty, towards the divine which is the slave to no thing. Either one makes use of this outer soul in order to be a transcendent object, being retired into oneself (κατὰ τοῦτο ζῆν ἀναχώρησις) or else one is deprived of the soul and lives in the bonds of Fatality.[51]

We are fortunate that the opinions of Stoic philosophers of the Hellenistic and Imperial periods, specifically regarding marriage and the philosophical life as distraction, have been preserved by the fifth century C.E. anthologist Stobaeus. In his *Anthologium* a chapter is included that divides the philosophers' views on marriage into three categories: (1) "marriage is best"; (2) "marriage is not good"; (3) "marriage is advantageous for some, not for others."[52] Although the inclusion of philosophers in partic-

---

[48]Porphyry, *Vit. Plot.* 22; 2.17.9.

[49]Festugière, *Personal Religion among the Greeks,* 65.

[50]*Enn.* 1.1.12,18.

[51]Ibid., 2.3.4.14-15.

[52]Cf. David L. Balch, "1 Cor. 7.32-35 and Stoic Debates About Marriage, Anxiety, and Distraction," *JBL* 102/3 (1983): 429-39, for discussion and for references in Stobaeus. Category 3 is liberally translated.

ular categories might now be questioned,[53] what is not questioned is the significance of the categories themselves as conclusions drawn by the philosophers about an issue that in effect served to betray certain views of the world or understandings of existence. The conclusions drawn about marriage served as an index of one's seriousness about, as well as ability to lead, the βίος φιλοσοφικός.

In the first category—"marriage is best"—a certain Antipater[54] is quoted:[55]

> But for a male who loves the good and wishes to lead a life of leisure devoted to reason or to political deeds or both, the matter is just the same. . . . The more he is turned away from household management, the more he must take a wife to do the housekeeping for him and make himself free from distraction (ἑαυτὸν ἀπερίσπαστον) about daily necessities.

In the second category—"marriage is not good"[56]—no *Stoic* philosopher is actually quoted, but Stobaeus could here have very appropriately included the topos on marriage in the Cynic—Stoic Epictetus:

> But in such an order of things as the present, which is like that of the battlefield, it is a question, perhaps if the Cynic ought not to be free from distraction (ἀπερίσπαστον), wholly devoted to the service of God.[57]

In the third category Epictetus's teacher, Musonius Rufus, is quoted:

> The husband and wife . . . should come together for the purpose of making a life in common and of procreating children, and furthermore of regarding all things in common between them, and nothing peculiar or private to one or the other, not even their own bodies . . . in marriage there must be above all perfect companionship and mutual love of husband and wife . . . under all conditions. . . . But where each looks only to his own interests and neglects the other, or, what is worse, when one is so minded and lives in the same house but fixes his attention elsewhere and is not

---

[53]Ibid., 434.

[54]Antipater of Tarsus, head of the Stoic school, ca. 130 B.C.E., or Antipater of Tyre, first century B.C.E.? See Balch, "1 Cor. 7.32-35," 432.

[55]From C. Wachsmuth and O. Hense, eds., *Anthologium*, 5 vols. (Berlin: Weidmann, 1958) 4.22; also in von Arnim, *SVF* 3.256,33–257,3, trans. Balch, "1 Cor. 7.32-35," 432.

[56]Cf. also 1 Cor. 7:1b.

[57]*Diss.* 3.22,69; cf. also 2.21, 22; 1.29, 59.

willing to pull together with his yoke-mate nor to agree, then the union is doomed to disaster.[58]

As for Paul, David Balch,[59] following C. K. Barrett, argues that his understanding of "anxiety" (μεριμνᾶν) in 1 Corinthians 7 is uniformly negative, and that his discussion parallels that of Musonius. According to Balch, for both Paul and Musonius marriage is neither good nor bad; it is, rather, good for some, not good for others, depending upon its anxiety-producing, distracting power. We have, however, already argued that μεριμνᾶν is *not* used in a uniformly negative way in 1 Corinthians 7, since it is qualified by objects that are diametrically opposed. So to the extent it is recognized that in Paul we have to do with a particular rhetorical use of the language of popular moral philosophy, to this extent only can it be argued that Musonius Rufus and Paul counseled much the same thing—one option good for some, bad for others, depending upon circumstances and effects. The goal for Paul, to be sure, was being able to handle the "distractions" of the world so that the Lord could be served. But the manner in which this goal is articulated is through the use of hyperbole (v. 32) and equivocation; these devices will not allow μεριμνᾶν to be uniformly negative. Like the uses of πάθος, πάθη, and ἀπάθεια in Greek moral philosophical discussions, μεριμνᾶν appears to be used by Paul in a very *playful* manner, carrying one meaning in one place, another meaning in another place.[60] Verse 32 clearly suggests the completely unequivocal negative aspect of μεριμνᾶν; verses 33-34, on the other hand, by virtue of the antithetical parallelism—τὰ τοῦ κυρίου, τὰ τοῦ κόσμου suggests the rather *neutral* understanding of μεριμνᾶν.

Paul does share with Epictetus an understanding of life-mission as a call that demands total dedication and sacrifice. Thus, for Paul as for Epictetus, the ideal might be to renounce marriage as anxiety producing. But

---

[58] 4.22.90, trans. from C. Lutz, *Musonius Rufus. The Roman Socrates,* Yale Classical Studies 10 (New Haven: Yale University Press, 1947) 88, 15-16.

[59] Balch, "1 Cor. 7:32-35," 434-35.

[60] N.B.: *hyperbole* with ἀμερίνους in v. 32a; equivocal use of μεριμνᾶν—change in connotative meaning from negative to positive in vv. 32b-34, the antithetical *stichoi*. Cf. discussion above, pp. 37-40, and John M. Rist, *Stoic Philosophy* (Cambridge: University Press, 1969) 25-26, 30-31, 34-35, 38, 45, 50, 52, 63, 72-73, 195-96, for a thorough discussion of formulations of Stoic philosophers (from Zeno and Chryssipus to late Stoa).

Paul is unwilling to counsel *all* the Corinthians to renounce marriage.[61] He, like Musonius Rufus, recognizes the importance of particular circumstances in the determination of what is appropriate and what is not, but neither bases teachings on universal circumstances (for example, being married).

The general affinity of Paul's advice with that of both Epictetus and Musonius Rufus, the sense that the general attitude towards marriage among the philosophers was an index of one's understanding of existence, and the tendency on the part of philosophers of the empire towards a spiritualizing ethic—these justify the drawing of parallels between Paul and Stoic philosophers of the Empire on the subject of spiritual and psychological detachment. Paul is in agreement with some philosophers that the ideal— devotion to the Lord (μεριμνᾶν τὰ τοῦ κυρίου —Paul), happiness (εὐδαιμονία—the philosophers)—is not dependent upon physical station or environment. Perhaps, beginning with Plato's articulation—but lost on many thereafter—this was an altogether new understanding of the religious life. Communion with divinity normally entailed some external expression of piety—cultic asceticism, a system of interdictions.[62]

The Stoic *summum bonum* was to be realized through a life of virtue. The latter was thought to consist of freedom from passions and from being disturbed by environment or the vicissitudes of life—ἀπάθεια. But, for the Stoic sage, this ἀπάθεια did not mean life completely devoid of passions or emotions, life without sympathy (συμπάθεια). The Stoic sage did not seek to be without feelings; he sought only to control them through reason. Freedom from passions was really only a negative first step. The ultimate goal was more positive—to replace passions with "rational feelings." It was, then, not ἀπάθεια so much as εὐπάθεια or μετριοπάθεια that was sought.[63]

---

[61]Note how, in 1 Cor. 7, he goes to great lengths to avoid giving a universal command. Cf. especially Καλὸν . . . δέ formulations.

[62]Emile Durkheim, *The Elementary Forms of Religious Life* (rpr.; New York: Free Press, 1965) 337-66; G. Van der Leeuw, *Religion in Essence and Manifestation,* 2 vols. (Gloucester MA: Peter Smith, 1967) 1:445-58.

[63]*SVF* 3.6, 15, 69.25; Ludwig Edelstein, *The Meaning of Stoicism* (Cambridge MA: Harvard University Press, 1966) 2; John M. Rist, "The Stoic Concept of Detachment," in *The Stoics,* John M. Rist, ed. (Berkeley: Univ. of California Press, 1978) 2; Rist, *Stoc Philosophy,* cf. n. 60.

For Paul the ideal was being able to concern oneself, without distur-
bance, with ''the things of the Lord.'' This entailed not renunciation of the
world, but engagement of the world under the coordinating influence of
passion for the Lord.

Both in Paul and among the philosophers can be discovered as a strategy for the realization of the respective goals a particular ''response to the
world.'' This response entailed acceptance of a hierarchy of values—the
realm of *ultimate* value(s) or concern, and the realm of *relative* values and
concerns. The realm of relative values—''the world''—was not despised
or rejected; it was engaged rationally, that is, with a view to the higher pursuit, to that which is good or appropriate in context. For the Stoics, this
meant an elaborate system for choosing among worldly things which ones
are appropriate (καθήκοντα, *officia*). For *Paul,* this meant counseling individuals according to their strengths and weaknesses and circumstances
(compare 7:1-28, 36-40). Within the sphere of relative values the Stoics
drew up criteria whereby some things—health, wealth, the honoring of
parents, attending the bedside of a sick friend, keeping promises, and so
forth—were ''promoted,'' ''preferred,'' but their opposites were ''de-
moted,'' ''devalued.''[64] Within the relative sphere of values, Paul—as the
whole of 1 Corinthians 7 indicates—counseled for and against the engagement of things worldly according to the individual's constitution and
the effects on community. There is no suggestion here that Paul shared the
actual goal of the Stoics. What was shared was the establishment of the
hierarchy of values—ultimate and relative—and the ''rational'' as opposed to anarchistic *engagement* of the world.

This ''rational'' approach was consonant with certain types of urban
experience. Max Weber has argued that in antiquity the religion of urban,
especially ''middle-class people''—including artisans—was characterized by a tendency towards the ordering and rationalizing of religious experience:

> the middle class, by virtue of its distinctive pattern of economic life, in-
> clines in the direction of a rational ethical religion. . . . When one com-
> pares the life of a lower-middle-class person, particularly the urban artisan
> or the small trader, with the life of the peasant, it is clear that middle-class
> life has far less connection with nature. Consequently, dependence on

---

[64]I. G. Kidd, ''Moral Actions and Rules in Stoic Ethics,'' in *The Stoics,* John M. Rist,
ed., 248-49.

magic for influencing the irrational forces of nature cannot play the same role for the urban dweller as for the farmer . . . the economic foundation of the urban man's life has a far more rational essential character, viz., calculability and capacity for purposive manipulation.[65]

The type of response to the world that this type of urban religious experience is likely to inspire Weber calls "inner-worldly asceticism." This orientation to the world involves participation in the world, an engagement of the institutions of the world, but without acceptance of the motives, presuppositions, and traditions of the world.

> The . . . worldly ascetic is a rationalist, not only in the sense that he rationally systematizes his own personal patterning of life, but also in his rejection of everything that is ethically irrational, esthetic, or dependent upon his own emotional reactions to the world and its institutions. The distinctive goal always remains the alert, methodical control of one's own pattern of life and behavior.[66]

In an analytical, comparative study of ancient and contemporary aristocratic societies and the social groups within them, John H. Kautsky[67] essentially upholds Weber's arguments regarding the orientation of the urban middle classes. The "townspeople," as he prefers to refer to urbanites— slaves, bureaucrats, priests, soldiers, entertainers, craftspeople, and so forth—were/are not *one* class but several, and respond differently to their situations. Those at the lowest level in the urban social ladder play no active role at all in politics or social policy. Others—bureaucrats, military, artists, scholars, magicians—are more directly economically and politically attached to, or dependent upon, the aristocracy. Such persons represent the aristocracy and carry out its orders. This group could hardly afford to challenge the *status quo* of which they are part. Still others are those townspeople who do play a very limited political role, but only in their own local spheres of interest. These are merchants and laborers organized in guilds who regulate recruitment, training, and benefits in their professions. They also represent and protect members vis-à-vis the aristocratic

---

[65]Max Weber, *The Sociology of Religion,* Ephraim Fischoff, trans., 4th ed. (Boston: Beacon Press, 1963) 97.

[66]Ibid., 166-68; quotation, 168.

[67]*The Politics of Aristocratic Empires* (Chapel Hill: University of North Carolina Press, 1982) cf. ch. 14, esp. 330-38.

bureaucracy regarding such matters as taxes, markets, and regulations. Although such groups on the whole have at best modest influence with the aristocratic bureaucracy, it is clear that they have contained the seeds for revolution. Eventually, only commercialization—the simultaneous development of technology and the nonaristocratic markets—liberates the townspeople from aristocratic hegemony.

The Stoic philosophers of the Empire, for the most part, should be placed in Kautsky's second category of townspeople. They were those who, by virtue of training and background, namely, the sharing of an aristocratic ethos, lived in close contact with the aristocracy. But unlike others who had access, they refused to place themselves in a situation of patronage and dependence—economic, political, or psychological. Above all, they wanted freedom to speak their minds on issues of the day. They did so in order to help engineer society in the direction they thought best. The authority for such office was vested in their calculated, "rational" renunciation of their world.[68]

The affinity between the stated view of Paul (ὡς μή) and some of the Stoic philosophers of the Empire (ἀπάθεια), and the "inner-worldly asceticism" of which Weber speaks, is clear.[69] In all cases there is engagement of the world in order to meet the ultimate goal. The world was to be overcome again and again through a rational ethic, a system of choosing between the things presented by the world. For the Stoics virtue is realized "in the midst of the battle," among choices between things deemed appropriate and not so; for Paul devotion to the Lord as the ultimate goal entailed a correct ordering and prioritizing of the things of the world.

Verse 35 is epexegetical of verses 32-34.[70] Σύμφορον ("benefit," "advantage") may have been employed by Paul in response to a real or imagined accusation.[71] As it is meant to be the opposite of the equally vague

---

[68]See MacMullen, *Enemies of the Roman Order,* 53-65.

[69]Wayne A. Meeks, *The First Urban Christians: The Social World of the Apostle Paul* (New Haven: Yale University Press, 1983) 84-107, characterizes the Pauline Christians' "response to the world" in terms of "tension" and "ambivalence." These terms square easily with Weber's "inner-worldly asceticism," and the spiritual detachment about which we have spoken.

[70]And, by logical extension, also of vv. 29-31. So the ὡς μή exhortations are being reinterpreted through v. 35.

[71]See Conzelmann, *1 Corinthians,* s.v., and Lietzmann, *An die Korinther,* s.v.

βρόχον ὑμῖν ἐπιβάλω ("cast a rope around your neck"), it was to imply that the counsel offered in 1 Corinthians 7 will prove to be no stumbling block. It is easy enough to imagine Paul anticipating the Corinthian rigorists arguing that his counsel, as a middle-of-the-road approach, could lead to disaster, that is, to compromise with the world. Paul is forced to argue that his way could bear fruit—more specifically, πρὸς τὸ εὔσχημον καὶ εὐπάρεδρον τῷ κυρίῳ ἀπερισπάστως ("to promote your good behavior and undistracted devotion to the Lord"). With the terms εὔσχημον, εὐπάρεδρον, ἀπερισπάστως, Paul betrays even more clearly the nature (model) of the ascetic behavior he commends to the Corinthians. It is a quality of "devotion" (τὸ εὐπάρεδρον) to the Lord that is at stake. The terms used to describe that quality of "devotion" suggest that Paul assumed not only that such would be experienced in the *social sphere*, within networks of relationships and activities, but also within a particular type of larger social location—the town or city. Regard for "propriety" (τὸ εὔσχημον),[72] and for "freedom from distraction" (ἀπερίσπαστος) was felt among (the Greco-Roman) urbanites, especially among the elite classes.[73]

Verse 35 further strengthens the argument regarding the affinity between Paul's counsel and the Stoic teaching on ἀπάθεια. The latter, as we have observed, also counseled realization of the goal through undistracted and proper deportment.

MEPIMNAN TA TOY KYPIOY = ᾿ΑΠΑΘΕΙΑ:
The Pauline Application of a Model of Ascetic Behavior

What Paul counsels in 1 Corinthians 7:32-35 is no outward change, not just because of the imminence of the end, but because of the principle on which he stands throughout 1 Corinthians 7—that a physical state or circumstance does not commend the Christian to God; only the keeping of the commands of God matters (v. 19). Whatever arguments might be mustered against particular efforts to change physical circumstances—the practice of celibacy within the bonds of marriage, divorce from an unbeliever—it remains for Paul that the major argument against such moves is

---

[72]Cf. Epictetus, *Diss.* 4.1.163.

[73]Cf. MacMullen, *Enemies of the Roman Order,* ch. 2; Salvatore Lilla, *Clement of Alexandria: A Study in Christian Platonism and Gnosticism* (Oxford: Oxford University Press, 1971) ch. 2.

the principle that such changes undermine the understanding of the nature and efficacy of God's work of salvation. If physical states or circumstances commend one to God, if celibacy makes one holy or pleasing to God, then one's salvation must depend upon such things, or at least one's orientation toward such things. Paul is careful to argue that since physical circumstances were irrelevant in one's coming into faith or salvation (v. 18), so also are they irrelevant as regards the maintenance of salvation or holiness.

But what *is* required is the attitude of the ὡς μή —spiritual withdrawal, detachment. The world itself is not evil, thus, no renunciation of it is required. But it does bring with it its own set of demands. It can be distracting. It makes claims, demands commitment (τὰ τοῦ κόσμου), the same kind of commitment the Lord requires (τὰ τοῦ κυρίου). As long as one is in the world desiring to be pleasing to the Lord, a tension or division of commitment ensues (μεμέρισται). One is torn between the world and "the things of the Lord." It is assumed by Paul that the supreme commitment must be to the Lord (v. 35). So what is required is inner detachment (ἀπάθεια), not physical withdrawal. Inner detachment is necessary because otherwise distraction and division will continue. What Paul recommends is a *relativizing* of all things in the world.

We know that by ὡς μή Paul cannot mean physical withdrawal, since throughout the chapter he has argued against any kind of change. Ὡς μή, then, must have to do with attitude. It is an "inner-worldly asceticism": the turning inward on the basis of self-disciplined commitment to transform the self in accord with the will of God. It is a rational form of renunciation which

> transforms the cathexis of the visionary from this world to higher things, not to renounce lowly things, but to put them in their proper place. Adolescent vision seeks to replace corrupted worldly matters by higher values; mature vision orders the world in terms of a proper relation of higher and lower things. By this vision of the whole the visionary attains insight into the hierarchy of being, clarifies his purpose, and achieves the steadfastness, the poise, and the good judgement of the spiritual state and worldly motives of other men, which makes the philosopher or the holy man indispensible to their societies.[74]

---

[74]Ira M. Lapidus, "Response to Peter Brown," in *Colloquy* 34 (Berkeley CA: Center for Hermeneutical Studies, 1980) 25.

Obviously, Paul's view about such existence in the world has import far beyond that which comes to expression in 1 Corinthians 7. The full import of his view can be understood only through analysis that would place the sentiment in a larger sociohistorical context, one that attempts not only to find clearer expression and application of this view as a model of existence within Pauline Christianity, but also to account for it over against other models of ascetic behavior as different responses to the Greco-Roman world. To this matter the next chapter is devoted.

◇——————————◆——————————◇

Chapter 4

῾ΩΣ ΜΗ as Response to the Urban Greco-Roman World

῾ΩΣ ΜΗ as Expression of "Response to the World"

The focal point at which Paul's view in 1 Corinthians 7 comes to expression is in the ὡς μή exhortations. With these exhortations and the interpretation applied to them in 1 Corinthians 7, Paul brings to expression his understanding of the appropriate Christian attitude toward the world.

Already this attitude has been described as a *relativizing* of all things worldly. The world is accepted as the sphere of Christian existence and obedience—but nothing more. The world has no power to legitimize or jeopardize Christian existence in itself. Just because the world is deemed ἀδιάφορον, the Christian is free to engage the world—in pursuit of "the things of the Lord." This engagement must entail a *reprioritizing* of concerns and cares (μεριμνᾶν) so that "the things of the Lord" are of ultimate concern. It is important to stress that Paul advocates engagement of the world, not spiritual anarchy or nihilism. He concedes the reality of the world as the sphere of Christian existence, counsels decision making about what things in the world are appropriate and what things are not. For example, he thinks sexual relations in the context of marriage appropriate on account of the dangers of πορνεία (v. 2). Single people and widows should get married if they find they cannot contain their sexual urges (Εἰ δὲ τις

ἀσχημονεῖν ἐπὶ τὴν παρθένον αὐτοῦ νομίζει, ἐὰν ᾖ ὑπέρακ-
μος, καὶ οὕτως ὀφείλει γίνεσθαι, ὃ θέλει ποιείτω· v. 36).[1]

British sociologist of religion Bryan R. Wilson[2] has drawn attention to
the fruitfulness of the study of religious movements—especially "minority" movements—in terms of the issues that 1 Corinthians 7:29-35 has
forced upon us, notably, that of a group's "response to the world." A
movement's "response to the world" has to do with the type of tension
that it has with its social environment. New, minority groups, by definition, reject the orthodox or dominant religious tradition and its worldview.
These groups must seek salvation in a way other than by acceptance of sec-
ular culture and orthodox religious tradition. What is designated "response to the world" may not always be located in the context of an
ongoing, stable, self-conscious movement. "Response to the world" may
manifest itself in all sorts of "unpurposive" activities, as well as in "purposive" lifestyle, associations, and doctrine.[3]

A group's "response to the world" may change with or without doc-
trinal changes. Changes in social circumstances, for example, mobility,
recruitment of a second generation, reactions of outsiders, the process of
institutionalization—these are more likely to effect change in a group's
"response to the world."

Wilson claims that attention to a group's "response to the world" can
facilitate both the comparative and dynamic dimensions of study of religions, since all social groups must engage the world in some respect—even
in some pattern—if they would distinguish themselves. It is important to
attempt to discover the *type* of engagement that marks a group in order to
understand its self-understanding.[4]

---

[1]The same advice is given to the parties referred to in vv. 25-28, 36-38 Apparently,
their celibacy involved special rigor. Perhaps they had taken vows. Paul's concern is to
emphasize the fact that if they could not handle the pressure of celibacy they could marry.
He stresses the fact that they do not sin if they marry (vv. 28, 36).

[2]*Magic and the Millennium* (New York: Harper & Row, Publishers, 1973) 16-30.

[3]Ibid., 18-20.

[4]Ibid., 21. Wilson might categorize the Pauline Christians' "response" as "conver-
sionist." Such "response," he argues, is cultivated in social conditions in which groups
are atomized, traditional social structures and relationships are impaired, or destroyed,
communities disrupted, and individuals often separated from their kinsfolk.

New Testament scholars in recent years have begun to study the social world of early Christianity with a view toward discovering, among other things, the nature of what Wayne Meeks refers to as the "collectivities" to which the earliest Christians belonged, and the "ordinary patterns of life in the immediate environment within which the Christian movement was born."[5] Interest in the social world, the "immediate environment" of the earliest Christians notwithstanding, very few New Testament scholars have made social orientation a specific and consistent heuristic device, or category of research, in the study of early Christianity.[6]

As the most recent comprehensive effort to describe and account for the significant segment of early Christianity called "Pauline Christianity"[7] through the employment of the methods and categories of the social sciences, Wayne Meeks's *The First Urban Christians* requires full consideration here. Meeks demonstrates interest not only in the *realia* of the social world of the first urban Christians, he is also interested in the *nature* of their "world," of their "symbolic universe," and in the ways in which they formed "world" vis-à-vis their environment. Meeks does not consistently or—as he would probably put it—slavishly make use of Bryan Wilson's categories. The closest Meeks comes to the kind of study that Wilson encourages appears in chapter 3 of his book ("The Formation of the *Ekklēsia*") in which he discusses the type of fellowship or association that the Pauline Christians formed. After comparing the fellowships of the Pauline Christians to various models in the contemporary environment, Meeks conclude that the models—the household, the voluntary association, the philosophical or rhetorical school, and the synagogue—all offer

---

[5]*The First Urban Christians* (New Haven: Yale University Press, 1983) 2.

[6]For a very useful state-of-the-discipline discussion, cf. A. J. Mahlerbe, *Social Aspects of Early Christianity*, 2nd ed. (Philadelphia: Fortress Press, 1983) 4-20; and Judge, "Antike und Christentum."

[7]In addition to Meeks's discussion regarding the limits of "Pauline Christianity" in *The First Urban Christians*, 7-8, see also Andreas Lindemann, *Paulus im ältesten Christentum: Das Bild des Apostels in der frühchristlichen Literatur bis Marcion* (Tübingen: J. C. B. Mohr, 1979); David Rensberger, "As the Apostle Teaches: The Development of the Use of Paul's Letters in Second-Century Christianity" (Ph.D. diss., Yale, 1981); Dennis R. MacDonald, *The Legend and the Apostle: The Battle for Paul in Story and Canon* (Philadelphia: Westminster Press, 1983).

important analogies, but none is to be seen as *the* model of the Christian ἐκκλησία.[8]

It is in terms of the "boundaries" that the Pauline churches drew between themselves and their social environment, especially, that Meeks approaches the kind of issue that has interested Wilson, as well as other sociologists and anthropologists. After a discussion of the indices for the drawing of boundaries in the Pauline communities, Meeks concludes that *tension* or *ambivalence* characterized their social orientation.[9] Full attention to his discussion of the evidence for the conclusion drawn about the group boundaries of the Pauline Christians is in order, not only because of its comprehensiveness, but also because such evidence will confirm the ὡς μή as an expression that captures the self-definition and pattern of behavior (social orientation) of the Pauline Christians. In other words, I expect the evidence regarding self-definition and pattern of behavior of the Pauline Christians to square with my argument regarding the nature of the counsel that ὡς μή signals.

Ὡς μή as Self-Definition and Pattern of Life in the Pauline Churches

The Pauline Christians formed fellowships with their own language patterns and set of meanings, beliefs, and authority. In the ways in which members of the community referred both to one another and to outsiders, they betrayed their self-understanding as a community or fellowship with boundaries.[10] In referring to one another with such terms and phrases as "saints" (ἅγιοι),[11] the "elect" (ἐκλήτοι),[12] those "known" by God,[13] "loved" by him,[14] "brothers" and "sisters,"[15] "children" (τέκνα),[16]

---

[8]Meeks, *The First Urban Christians,* 74-84.

[9]Ibid., 84-107.

[10]Ibid., 84-85.

[11]1 Cor. 1:2; 2 Cor. 1:1; Phil. 1:1; Rom. 1:7; Eph. 1:1; Col. 1:2.

[12]1 Thess. 1:14; Rom. 8:33; Col. 3:12; 1 Cor. 1:27; Eph. 1:4.

[13]1 Cor. 8:3; Gal. 4:9.

[14]Rom. 1:7, Col. 3:12; 1 Thess. 1:4; 2 Thess. 2:13.

[15]"My brothers" (ἀδελφοί) appears over sixty times in the authentic Pauline letters; the term may be peculiar to Paul, so Meeks argues, 87.

[16]Gal. 4:19; 1 Cor. 4:14; 2 Cor. 6:13; 12:14; also "children of God," Rom. 8:16, 21; 9:8; Phil. 2:15.

"the body of Christ,"[17] "the body,"[18] the members of the community were demonstrating their solidarity, their consciousness of being an ἐκκλησία. They were the "Church of God,"[19] "the Lord's Church,"[20] "Jesus Christ's,"[21] "God's and Christ's,"[22] the "Israel of God,"[23] the "true sons of Abraham,"[24] the "holy nation,"[25] the "people of God."[26]

This community had *common beliefs and experiences*. They all had "turned to God from idols, to serve a living and genuine God" (1 Thess. 1:9). None of them believed in the so-called "gods" and "lords" of the Gentiles; all confessed belief in "one God, the Father, from whom are all things and for whom all things exist, and one Lord, Jesus Christ, through whom are all things and through whom we exist" (1 Cor. 8:5-6). They all believed in the uniqueness of the revelation that they had received concerning the significance of Jesus' death as the Christ and his resurrection.[27]

---

[17]1 Cor. 12:12-13.

[18]See Robert Gundry, *SŌMA* in *Biblical Theology: With Emphasis on Pauline Anthropology* (Cambridge: Cambridge University Press, 1976) for the most recent comprehensive discussion of use of term in Paul; see Meeks, *The First Urban Christians,* 90, regarding the Pauline school's extension and elaboration of the metaphor.

[19]1 Cor. 1:2; 2 Cor. 1:1; Ignatius, *Eph., Mg., Tr., Phld.; 1 Clem. pr.;* 1 Cor. 10:32; 11:22; 15:9; Gal. 1:13.

[20]Acts 20:28; 1 Tim 3:5, 16; *Did.* 9:4; 10:5; 11:11; Hermas, *Vis.* 1.1,6; 3.4; *Sim.* 8.6,4; 9.13,1; 18.2; *Barn.* 7:11; *2 Clem.* 2:1; 14:1-4.

[21]*Eph.* 5:1 (Ignatius).

[22]Ign. *Phld., pr., Sm. pr.*

[23]Gal. 6:16.

[24]Rom. 9:7-8; Gal. 4:22-23.

[25]*Barn.* 14:6; 1 Pet. 2:9.

[26]Heb. 4:9; 10:30; Rev. 18:14; 1 Clem 59:4; Herm., *Sim.* 5.5,3.

[27]Meeks, *The First Urban Christians,* 92. For other discussions of the issue from different perspectives, cf. David Wenham, "The Christian Life: A Life of Tension—A Consideration of the Nature of Christian Experience in Paul," *Pauline Studies: Essays Presented to Professor F. F. Bruce on his 70th Birthday,* Donald A. Hagner and Murray J. Harris, eds., 1st American ed. (Grand Rapids: Wm. B. Eerdmans Publishing Co., 1980) 80-84; James D. G. Dunn, *Jesus and the Spirit: A Study of the Religious and Charismatic Experience of Jesus and the First Christians as Reflected in the New Testament* (Philadelphia: Westminster Press, 1975) 301-42.

Through their *rituals* the members of the community also betrayed their solidarity and church consciousness. Baptism served as the rite of initiation into the community. Those who wished to become a part of the community had to be "washed" and "sanctified" (1 Cor. 6:11; Rom. 6). Baptism represented a "taking off" of the old ἄνθρωπος and the "putting on" of the new ἄνθρωπος. The Lord's Supper, too, defined fellowship. It signified membership in the community.[28]

Other institutions created by the community to meet needs that otherwise would have to be met by outsiders also reinforced the sense of community. The communal meals, court procedures to adjudicate civil disputes between members, and fellowship itself are examples.[29]

The other side of community formation and solidarity is separateness or delimitation from outsiders.[30] The Pauline Christians referred to those not among them as "outsiders" (οἱ ἔξω),[31] "the world," or "this world,"[32] "non-believers" (ἄπιστοι),[33] "those who do not know God,"[34] "children of darkness."[35]

Separation involved exclusion from other cults. Involvement with such belongs to "the time that is past."[36] Exclusion is important because the other cults practice sorcery[37] and magic and invoke demons.[38]

---

[28]Meeks, *The First Urban Christians,* 102-103, 150-63; cf. Gal. 2:11-14; 3:26-27; 1 Cor. 5:11; 6:1-8; 10:15-22; 11:29-30; Rom. 6; Col. 2:12.

[29]Meeks, *The First Urban Christians,* 103-105.

[30]Ibid., 94-95.

[31]1 Cor. 5:12-13; 1 Thess. 4:12; Col. 4:5.

[32]1 Cor. 1:20-21; 2:12; 3:19; 5:10; 6:2; 7:31; 33-34; 11:32; Gal. 4:3; 6:14; Eph. 2:2; Col. 2:8, 20.

[33]1 Cor. 6:6; 7:12-13; 10:27; 14:22-23; 2 Cor. 4:4; 6:14.

[34]1 Thess. 4:5; Gal. 4:8; 2 Thess. 1:8.

[35]1 Pet. 4:3; *Barn.* 16:7; *2 Clem.* 17:1.

[36]Bultmann, *Theology,* 1:99; cf. especially 2 Cor. 6:14-7:1; also 1 Cor. 10:1-22; 5:10-11; 6:9; Gal. 5:20; Rev. 21:8; 22:15; *Did.* 3:4; 5:1; *Barn.* 20:1.

[37]Bultmann, *Theology,* 1:100; *Barn.* 16:7; 1 Cor. 10:20-21.

[38]1 Cor. 3:16-17; 2 Cor. 6:16; Eph. 2:21-22; 1 Pet. 2:5; 1 Tim. 3:15; Heb. 3:6; 10:21; Ignatius, *Eph.* 9:1; *Mg.* 7:2; Herm., *Sim.* 9.13,9; 14, 1.

Separation included the whole of the reality outside the community—
the world—on account of its moral uncleanness and shortcomings. The
pure, sanctified members of the community are exhorted to cleanse themselves,[39] to be careful not to conform to the ways of the heathen,[40] to remain "unstained" from the world.[41] In the midst of "a crooked and
perverse generation" the members of the community must be "blame-
less," "innocent."[42] They are called to "forsake . . . this world, and do
the will of him who called us, and not fear to go forth from this world."[43]
They must "bid farewell to this world to consort with the one to come."[44]

Of course, what we are confronted with here is the *rhetoric* or *language* of renunciation. What needs to be clarified is the relationship between the *language* of renunciation and the *practice* of renunciation. The
separation that was realized did not entail a going out of the world. What
was involved was a critique and rejection of the ways (σχῆμα) of the world,
of its ethos, not the physical world itself. What was rejected were the lusts
and passions and cares of the world. These were to be abstained from.[45]
The Pauline Christians were expected to "cast off the works of darkness,"
that is, put aside the vices of greed and passions.[46] What was demanded
was not otherworldly asceticism, not physical abstention, but a type of *inner*-worldly (spiritual) renunciation. There was no consistent or mass effort either to go out of the world or to participate in and affirm the world.

---

[39]2 Cor. 7:1; 1 Pet. 1:14; Eph. 4:17.

[40]James 1:27; 2 Pet. 3:14, Rom. 12:1-2.

[41]Phil. 2:15; 1 Pet. 2:12.

[42]*2 Clem.* 5:1, meaning to lead a holy and righteous life, and to regard the things of this
world as not our own, and not desire them (*2 Clem.* 5:6); cf. Ignatius, *Rom.* pr.; Herm.,
Sim. 1.3 and 11.

[43]*2 Clem* 6:3-4.

[44]Bultmann, *Theology,* 1:104; cf. Rom. 1:24; Titus 2:12; 1 Pet. 2:11; *Did.* 1:4; Gal.
5:16, 24; Eph. 2:3; *1 Clem.* 28; especially, Herm., *Vis.* 3.11,3; *Vis.* 1.3.1; *Mand.* 5.2,2;
10:1,4; *Vis.* 3.6,5; *Sim.* 8.8,1-2; 9.20,1-2 for exhortations against cares and occupations
of the world, of daily living.

[45]ἀπέχεσθαι : 1 Thess. 4:3; 5:22; 1 Pet. 2:11; *Did.* 1:4; Herm., *Mand.* 11.8; 12.1,3;
2.2; 7.3.

[46]ἀποθέσθαι: Rom. 13:12; 1 Thess. 5:8; Eph. 6:11, 14; Col. 3:12; Herm. *Vis.* 4.1,8;
Mand. 2.3-4; 5.2,8; 9.7 and 10; 10.3,1 and 4; 11.4; 12.1,1; 2,4; *Sim.* 6.1,2 and 4; 5,3;
8.9,1; 9.29,3; Ign., *Polyc.* 1.2.

The world was seen as ἀδιάφορον. Salvation required neither the embracing of, nor flight from, the world.

Meeks[47] points to two concrete examples of efforts on the part of the Pauline Christians to come to grips with the most appropriate ways of engaging the world. The issues—sexual relations and idolatry—are especially important because they are seen to be treated by Paul in enough detail to justify the conclusion to which Meeks is drawn regarding Paul's and the Pauline Christians' social orientation.[48]

Interaction between Christians and non-Christians was at issue in the questions posed by the Corinthians regarding "meat offered to idols" (1 Cor. 8:1). Paul's response was an ambivalent one in the sense that, on the one hand, social intercourse with outsiders is not prohibited, the act of eating meats known to have been offered to idols was desacralized and was not in itself proscribed. Eating or not eating—both are ἀδιάφορα (8:8). On the other hand, there were strict proscriptions against participation in any other cult.

Similarly, Paul's response to questions about marriage and sex were found by Meeks to be *ambivalent*. Meeks sees 1 Thess. 4:1-8, in addition to 1 Cor. 7 (vv. 1-16!), as a key passage. Paul's admonitions were full of exaggerated descriptions of the "impurity" and πορνεία of the outside world (cf. 1 Thess. 4:3-8). Members of the church communities were called, on the one hand, to "holiness" (separation), life in accord with a different code of conduct.[49] On the other hand, Paul does not categorically dissuade Christians who are married to nonbelievers to separate from

---

[47]*The First Urban Christians*, 97-102.

[48]Of course, it is doubly significant for our purposes that of the texts Meeks investigates (1 Cor. 7-10), the passage that has been our concern is included. Of the two case-examples Meeks deems significant for an understanding of the Pauline Christians' social orientation, that of marriage and sex is included. I see further significance in the issue dealing with marriage and sex in 1 Cor. 7:29-35 in that here Paul attempts to give a *rationale* for his teachings, to posit an overarching principle for his position.

[49]Cf. also 1 Cor. 6:9; Rom. 1:26-27; Gal. 5:9; Eph. 5:3; Col. 3:5. Meeks, *The First Urban Christians*, 100-101, thinks that the manner in which the admonitions about marriage and morality were formulated ("not as the Gentiles who do not know God") suggests the code of conduct of the diaspora synagogue as the tradition of origins. But he and other scholars have come to recognize that the rhetoric of the moral superiority of the Jews and Christians of the period did not reflect an accurate picture of pagan society, as the "pagan" novelists and moralists attest. Cf. ch. 3, nn. 135, 136.

them—for whatever reasons. Nor does he unequivocally support sexual aseticism.

Meeks concludes, using the categories advanced by Mary Douglas, that the language and concrete issues discussed above serve as evidence of the relatively open or *ambivalent* social boundaries of the Pauline churches. The Pauline Christians had *both* a strong sense of belonging to a special community with its own language patterns, beliefs, rituals, and institutions, *and* a sense of separateness from the world "outside the gates." They remained in the towns in which their communities were founded and continued to "use the world." Paul rejects any effort to make Christian existence radically otherworldly (1 Cor. 5:9-10). This would be absurd and self-defeating, since it would render mission—an important concern—impossible, and give outsiders a bad impression.[50]

Beyond the concrete examples to which Meeks points, the manner in which Paul handles the situation involving Philemon and Onesimus is also instructive. It shows how slavery as an example of a worldly condition or status was viewed by Paul. The condition of slavery was in itself not of concern; all that seemed to matter was the ability of Onesimus to enjoy status as a "beloved brother," "as a slave but more than a slave . . . both in the flesh and in the Lord" (v. 16), so that the community's concord and integrity could be maintained. Paul does not speak to the issue of the rightness or wrongness of slavery, or any other issue or structure of society. He is concerned simply with the individual's response to his or her situation—which may be alterable (1 Cor. 7:21).

In a recently published study[51] of Philemon in which the categories and insights of anthropologist Victor Turner are much employed, Norman Petersen argues that Paul's lack of (moral) concern regarding the master-slave relationship, along with other worldly distinctions and relationships—Jews and "Greeks," male and female—betrays his and his churches' *accommodation* to the "structures" of the world, on the one hand. The *basis* of

---

[50]Ibid., 105-106. See Also W. C. van Unnik, "Die Rucksicht auf die Reaktion der NichtChristen als Motiv in der altchristlichen Paraenese," in *Judentum, Urchristentum, Kirche: Festschrift für Joachim Jeremias,* Walther E. Eltester, ed. (Berlin: Verlag Alfred Töpelmann, 1960) 221-33. About these two considerations in connection with social status origins, see more below.

[51]*Rediscovering Paul: Philemon and the Sociology of Paul's Narrative World* (Philadelphia: Fortress Press, 1985).

the accommodation to the "structures" of the world, on the other hand, is "antistructural."[52]

> Paul's principle of not changing the marks of [worldly] distinction is not in itself antistructural but its basis is, for he argues that in the church "neither circumcision counts for anything nor uncircumcision, but keeping the commandment's of God" (1 Cor. 7:19). Thus, the church's practice is antistructurally opposed to a social structural distinction obtaining outside of the church. . . . Male and female, Jew and Gentile, slave and free comprise three sets of fundamental social structural distinctions that Paul sees in the world and that he also sees as antistructurally opposed in the church.

The ambivalence about which Meeks speaks as regards Paul and the Pauline Christians' social orientation, Petersen casts in a similar language. The acceptance of some of the distinctions and particular structures and relationships of the world *within* the church (e.g., marriage, family, slavery, ethnic differences), represents acknowledgment that the church *spatially* exists within the world. But the rejection of many of the presuppositions of the "structures" of the world and the introduction of real differences (or refinements) within those structures (e.g., temporary celibacy for married couples, celibate marriages) represent the ascetic antistructural nature of the movement.

Again, it is most significant that this conclusion about the Pauline Christians' social *orientation* is drawn only after much attention to 1 Corinthians 7. Both Meeks and Petersen have seen the importance of the case issue[53] of marriage and sex as an index of the Pauline Christians' understanding of themselves in the world. But neither has seen the significance of the ὡς μή passage as Paul's deliberate attempt to articulate more fully and clearly both the nature of Pauline Christians' response to the world, and the reigning principle behind it. This argument assumes the heuristic significance of the passage.

---

[52]Ibid., 155-56.

[53]For our purposes, discussion of the responses of the Pauline Christians to every aspect of life in the Greco-Roman world is not important here. Far more important is the establishment of a *pattern* of responses. Enough case examples have been discussed to establish the pattern for which ὡς μή is an expression. Indeed, this entire study represents careful attention to one case-example and the articulated principle behind it. For survey approaches see Ernst Troeltsch, *The Social Teachings of the Christian Churches,* vol. 1, Olive Wyon, trans. (New York: Macmillan, 1931; rpr.: University of Chicago Press, 1931); Robert M. Grant, *Early Christianity and Society: Seven Studies* (San Francisco: Harper & Row, 1977).

ʹΩΣ ΜΗ as Aristocratic Urban Spirituality: The Heuristic Significance of 1 Corinthians 7:29-35

Our exegetical chapters have already established the ὡς μή exhortations as expressive of a model of ascetic behavior that can be variously described as "inner-worldly" (Weber), "spiritual retirement" (Festugière), "psychological detachment," ἀπάθεια, "ambivalence" (Meeks), or "antistructural" (Petersen). This "response to the world" could be—in fact, has been—detected and isolated without careful attention to 1 Corinthians 7:29-31. But 1 Corinthians 7:29-31 is significant beyond providing one further case example of the "response." It is *heuristically* significant in a number of respects.

1. It represents one of the earliest self-conscious attempts on the part of any early Christian writer, certainly any New Testament writer, to clarify and provide a rationale for Christian attitudes toward the world. Although the New Testament is a virtual textbook of social precepts, and although the Pauline correspondence is outstanding in the New Testament in this regard, there are very few self-conscious remarks made about Christian existence in the world, regarding the actual pattern or *model* of existence, or the influential factors and issues behind such a model.

What we encounter in 1 Corinthians 7-10 is part of a dialogue carried on by Paul and some of those who have become Christians through the work of the Pauline mission. The discussion has to do with specific, practical matters, and in 1 Corinthians 7, Paul, being the pastor/teacher he was,[54] quickly moved to indicate how such matters relate to Christian calling and existence in general. In order to do this he had to provide a *principle* upon which his advice about specific, practical matters could be based. Thus, the ὡς μή exhortations. They not only describe the *model* of Christian existence in the world Paul deems appropriate, but also the *rationale* behind this model. In no other passage does Paul *directly* address these matters.

2. The larger context of discussion in which the ὡς μή model is included also alludes to other *models* of Christian existence.

Since our exegesis of 1 Corinthians 7:29-35 had as its goal an understanding of the function of the ὡς μή exhortations, it had first to come to certain conclusions about the origin of verses 29-31. We concluded that

---

[54]See Werner Wolbert, *Ethische Augmentation und Paranese in 1 Kor. 7* (Duesseldorf: Patmos-Verlag, 1981).

the passage had its origin in the context of eschatological prophecy regarding the imminence of the End. For his purposes in responding to the Corinthians' questions, Paul shifts the emphasis away from the imminence motif to the transitoriness of the world and its distracting power. Already here is evidence of diversity and development in early Christian social orientation. Paul takes up the eschatological prophecy as an understanding of existence (and as traditional material). He does not reject the notion of the imminence of the End; he de-emphasizes its importance. It becomes an ancillary rather than dominating factor in terms of the Christian model of existence in the world. What is alone determinative for the model of Christian existence is the capacity to pursue "the things of the Lord."

Behind the traditional material that Paul takes up in the ὡς μή passage is the apocalyptic "loss of world."[55] Again, Paul does not reject this view, he reinterprets it. What he does reject are the other understandings of existence in the world that are alluded to in 1 Corinthians 7.[56]

First, in verses 17-24—the first use of expanded analogies in the chapter—in order to make this point regarding the importance of "remaining" in the social status or condition in which one was called by God, Paul uses circumcision and uncircumcision as two of the examples of worldly condition or status. (Circumcision and uncircumcision are, in addition, examples of religious status. Circumcision was regarded by Jews as a mark of purity that separated them from pagans. Paul here sets aside this and—we are meant to understand—all other marks of purity, or religious status.[57]) They are all unimportant as regards Christian existence; what matters is the keeping of the commandments of God (v. 19).

Second, it is clear throughout the chapter that Paul is reacting to the Corinthians' questions. His responses betray his understanding that these questions are part of a perhaps still-developing understanding in Corinth of Christian existence in the world that makes escape from the world a requirement. As has been pointed out in chapters one and two above, throughout 1 Corinthians 7 Paul argues against this understanding. His counsel on remaining is a response to the Corinthians' notion that the world, that is, worldly status or condition, can ill affect one's status with God. To

---

[55]See James M. Robinson, "World in Theology and in New Testament Theology," 107.

[56]See the discussion in ch. 1, pp. 21-22 above.

[57]See Meeks, *The First Urban Christians*, 91-92, 103.

this Paul answers "remain"—not because remaining in itself commends one to God, but only because the Corinthians appear to think that they can reach spiritual perfection through flight from the world. They apparently understood themselves as the spiritually elite—those who not only know what is required of the spiritually perfect, but also are endowed so as to be able to endure, in this case, the ascetic rigor that perfection requires.

First Corinthians 7, then, contains evidence for the existence of at least four different early Christian understandings of existence in the world. (1) Through the employment and reinterpretation of the ὡς μή exhortations Paul brings to expression his own understanding of Christian existence in the world, and thereby gives evidence for another understanding—(2) *apocalyptic spirituality* (vv. 29-31a). Of course, the entire chapter is a response to (3)*the ascetic-leaning questions raised by some of the Corinthian believers*. Behind their questions Paul reads an understanding of Christian existence. In the course of his effort to respond to such questions (chapters 7-15) Paul makes use of analogies as foils for his argument. One of these analogies points to yet another understanding of Christian existence—(4) *cultic*, or *ritual markers*.[58] Ritual markers are not at issue in 1 Corinthians 7, and probably not in Corinth at the time of writing of 1 Corinthians.

The larger question that remains is the *historical* relationship between the "understandings" isolated above. But the immediate question before us is the *heuristic suggestiveness* of the expressions of these "understandings" in 1 Corinthians 7. The ὡς μή exhortations must remain the focal point of investigation, since they express not only Paul's view, but also the *basis* of his responses to other "understandings" of Christian existence in the world. It is important first to determine the "world" that comes to expression through κόσμος in 1 Corinthians 7 and the "world" in evidence in the Pauline churches generally. Such information would be most helpful in the effort to clarify the nature of the diversity of early Christianity.

3. The larger context of discussion in which the ὡς μή exhortations are found also provides direct and indirect information regarding some of the *factors* that account for the Pauline churches' attention to the model of ascetic behavior of which the exhortations are an expression.

---

[58]Ibid., 92, 97-98, 103.

a. Certainly basic to Paul and to the Pauline mission was the conviction that the Parousia was imminent.[59] This conviction was no mere item of dogma that could be abstracted; it was the event that articulated the hopes and self-understandings of the early Christians.[60] It reminded them of their common heritage and destiny and thereby had the mythic power to establish a baseline of authority for ethical behavior and social orientation.[61] The Parousia did not always dictate the same pattern of behavior in the world. The invocation of eschatological or apocalyptic prophecy did not always presuppose a particular model of social behavior. Paul himself used such language at different times to commend different views and models of social and personal behavior.[62]

Diversity of functions of the language regarding the Parousia notwithstanding, the eschatological language employed in 1 Corinthians 7:29-31 admonished a type of renunciation of the world that Paul feels the need to reinterpret and reapply for the Corinthians. This suggests that Paul had come to associate traditional eschatological prophecy in general with admonition toward radical, or physical renunciation of the world (cf. 2 Thess. 3:7-12, especially v. 10). Paul's employment of eschatological prophecy in 1 Corinthians 7, notwithstanding his pastoral need to reinterpret and reapply it, further suggests that he thought, in agreement with some of the Corinthians, that *some form of "taking out of the world," of renunciation,* was *fundamental to Christian existence.*

Throughout 1 Corinthians 7 Paul attempts to indicate the problems he has with the Corinthians' views. In employing the eschatological prophecy in order finally to articulate his own views (vv. 29-35), Paul rejects both the Corinthian model and another model (apocalyptic) that he himself introduces through his *modification* of both. Whatever the reasons for the model of renunciation that Paul commends for Christian existence, such a model cannot be equated with the Corinthians' absolutist renunciation of the world expressed through rejection of the most basic structures and as-

---

[59]See the discussion in ch. 2 above.

[60]See Ernst Käsemann, ''On the Subject of Primitive Christian Apocalyptic,'' *New Testament: Questions of Today,* W. J. Montague, trans. (London: SCM Press, Ltd.; Philadelphia: Fortress, 1969) 108-38; J. Christiaan Beker, *Paul the Apostle,* pt. 3; cf. ch. 2 above.

[61]See Meeks, *The First Urban Christians,* 174-75; Beker, *Paul the Apostle,* 272.

[62]Meeks, *The First Urban Christians,* 171-80.

sociations of the world, or reduced simply to the convictions that "the time is short."

b. The employment of the language resonant of moral philosophy points both to the larger social setting (urban) and at least to social status *incli-nations* and *proclivities* (aristocratic), if not origins, as factors in the rein-terpretation of the eschatological-prophetic, and absolutist-pneumatic models of renunciation. Employment of the language of "moral restraint"[63] in 1 Corinthians 7:32-35, especially as it follows as reinterpretation of the eschatological prophecy in verses 29-31, suggests *class-specific* influence, perhaps, even a class-specific attitude towards the world. If we were correct in associating the language and sentiment of 1 Corinthians 7:32-35 with the aristocratic classes of the empire—especially the Stoic philosophers—we can reasonably argue that as a leader of the Pauline mission, Paul betrayed the aristocratic influences on his moral and ethical views and teachings, the social constitution of the believers notwithstanding.[64]

We have already argued the Greco-Roman philosophical *topos* of ἀπάθεια as the intellectual-social context for Paul's discussion in 1 Corinthians 7:32-35. The issue about which the philosophers and moralists of the Hellenistic Roman periods were concerned was the appropriate attitude towards the world for the lover of wisdom. 'Απάθεια was often miscon-strued as Stoic advocacy of complete indifference, a state of passionless-ness. But in the Empire philosophers understood ἀπάθεια as a radically different reorientation to the world, with a different set of priorities—all effected by a *psychological, spiritual distancing* from the world. This spir-itual distancing functioned as social criticism in the sense that it implied that society was less then ideal as an environment for the seeker of truth and wisdom.

Paul was commending a similar attitude toward the world in 1 Corin-thians 7:29-35. 'Αμέριμνος was the term he used, which functioned in much the same way as ἀπάθεια among the Stoic philosophers. The man-ner in which Paul goes on to qualify the term indicates his concern to com-mend a psychological-spiritual detachment from society so that a total reorientation to society under the reigning interpretive concern regarding "things of the Lord" could be realized.

---

[63]See Helen North, *Sophrosyne* (Ithaca NY: Cornell University Press, 1966) esp. chs. 7, 8, 9.

[64]See Meeks, *The First Urban Christians*, 51-73, cf. 1 Cor. 1:26.

This spiritual detachment could and did assume different reifications. The Pauline Christians collected themselves into local communities (κατ' οἶκον ἐκκλησία) in which they sought to realize the new orientation. The philosophers, on the whole, remained rugged individualists. The world was "used" by both the Paulinists and the philosophers, but from different social-status *platforms*.

The *aristocratic* philosophers shared the general ethos of the aristocratic classes.[65] Their "asceticism" was intended not as a total rejection of the culture, but as an investment in the improvement of the self. The perpetual distancing from the world was meant to aid the lover of wisdom in the struggle against those universal enemies of truth and wisdom that keep the great majority of the culture from gaining wisdom.

Yet, the world was not abandoned by these philosophers. They were often found in courts and palaces, preaching and exhorting. As aristocrats they were generally supportive of a benevolent monarchy. What was demanded was that the monarch be wise, rational, temperate, and just.[66] These philosophers were even willing to show, in their own lives as models, how the emperor should rule.[67] They were defining themselves as examples of cultural virtue. Seneca sums up the attitude:

> I myself would not deny that sometimes one must retire (*cedendum*), but it should be a gradual retreat without surrendering the standards, without surrendering the honour of a soldier; those are more respected by their enemies and safer who come to terms with their arms in their hands. This is what I think Virtue and Virtue's devotee should do. If Fortune shall get the upper hand and shall cut off the opportunity for action, let a man not straightway turn his back and flee, throwing away his arms and seeking some hiding place, as if there were anywhere a place where Fortune could

---

[65]See Peter Brown, "The Philosopher and Society in Late Antiquity," in *Protocol of the Thirty-Fourth Colloquy of the Center for Hermeneutical Studies*, Edward C. Hobbs and Wilhelm Wuellner, eds (Berkeley CA: The Center for Studies in Hellenistic and Modern Culture, 1980) passim.

[66]See Ramsay MacMullen, *Enemies of the Roman Order* (Cambridge MA: Harvard University Press, 1966) 62: In Rome, especially, philosophy corresponded to the prejudices of social classes. Aristocratic Stoics upheld the "ideal" of the monarchy, checked by the senate and local magistrates. Cynics were more prone to preach anarchy. Cf. also Seneca's *Ad Polyb., De clem., De benef., Ep.* 73, and Dio's discourses on kingship.

[67]MacMullen, *Enemies of The Roman Order*, 51-52, cf. Seneca, *Ep.*, 39; Chion of Heraclea, *Epp.*, 12, 13; Dio, *Or*, 20.26, Diog. Laert., 7.130.

not reach him, but let him devote himself to his duties more sparingly, and, after making choice, let him find something in which he may be useful to the state. Is he not permitted to be a soldier? Let him help his countrymen by his silent support. Is it dangerous even to enter the forum? In private houses, at the public spectacles, at feasts, let him show himself a good comrade, a faithful friend, a temperate feaster. Has he lost the duties of a citizen? Let him exercise those of a man. The very reason for our magnanimity in not shutting ourselves up within the walls of one city, in going forth into intercourse with the whole earth, and in claiming the world as our country, was that we might have a wider field for our virtue. . . . If Fortune has removed you from the foremost position in the state, you should, nevertheless, stand your ground and help with the shouting, and if someone stops your throat, you should, nevertheless, stand your ground and help in silence. The service of a good citizen (*opera civis boni*) is never useless; by being heard and seen, by his expression, by his gesture, by his silent stubbornness, and by his very walk (*incessuque ipso*) he helps.[68]

Of course, the social status of the Pauline Christians was not aristocratic. I accept the present scholarly mixed-status-majority-skilled-worker (artisan) consensus regarding the social status of early Christians.[69] I am attracted to Meeks's argument that many in the Pauline circles (including Paul himself) can be typed as people of "high status inconsistency." "Upwardly mobile . . . their achieved status [was] higher than their attributed status."[70]

Ronald Hock's work[71] on Paul's ministry in the social context of the skilled worker (as a tentmaker) does not contradict the status-inconsistency argument, but lends it support. It also helps account for the type of language in 1 Corinthians 7:32-35. Hock's observations about the opinions that the artistocratic classes held about skilled work and workers in general,[72] about Paul's exhortations to members of his churches to work hard, live in seemly fashion (εὐσχημόνως) toward outsiders, and to live

---

[68]*De tranq.*, iv.1-6.

[69]Cf. Malherbe, *Social Aspects of Early Christianity*, 29-59; Gerd Theissen, *Social Setting of Pauline Christianity*, John Schütz, ed. and trans. (Philadelphia: Fortress, 1982) ch. 2.

[70]Meeks, *The First Urban Christians*, 73.

[71]*The Social Context of Paul's Ministry: Tentmaking and Apostleship* (Philadelphia: Fortress, 1980), esp. 26-49.

[72]Ibid., 35-37.

quietly,[73] suggest that Paul was reflecting the class origins of the majority of his converts—the urban working class and poor—but was seeking to gain the attention and approval of those outside these circles, namely, the urban aristocratic classes.

In 1 Corinthians 7:32-35 Paul employs language that is intended to effect much the same response to the world (note: even εὐσχημον in v. 35!). Paul wants the Corinthians to adopt an attitude towards the world that would commend them as responsible social beings, even as they attempt to reflect their new set of priorities in the life of faith.

Given their nonaristocratic status in society, it was never likely that the Pauline Christians would ever consciously attempt to reform the society in which they lived. As folk already not "at home"[74] in the empire, they could only be guided in the direction first of accepting the basic structures of the world as an acceptable framework for their new existence. Paul should be read in 1 Corinthians 7:32-35 as the leader of the new community who attempts to guide the community in the direction of accepting the world as the *sphere* of Christian existence. This same community, perhaps this same leader, could not have realized much more than this (e.g., the social-engineering, social-activist posture).[75]

The attitude on the part of Paul and his churches towards the political and social life, as Ernst Troeltsch puts it, and as our exegesis confirms, "stops short at the borders of the value of the spiritual life and the church community."[76] But Troeltsch may also be correct in arguing that this attitude on the part of Paul and his churches had potential for more positive influence beyond the church community.

> It is a more remarkable thing that the entirely revolutionary and radical principle of unlimited individualism and universalism should adopt such a thoroughly conservative attitude to social questions. In spite of this, however, it actually exercised a revolutionary influence. For the conservative

---

[73]Ibid., 42-47; cf. 1 Thess. 4:10b-12.

[74]Cf. John H. Elliott, *A Home for the Homeless: A Sociological Exegesis of 1 Peter, Its Situation, and Strategy* (Philadelphia: Fortress, 1981). Certainly the major thesis regarding "homelessness" is applicable to Paul's generation.

[75]This is what otherwise perceptive critics such as historican G. E. M. de Ste. Croix fail to see. Cf. his *The Class Struggle in the Ancient Greek World: From the Archaic Age to the Arab Conquests* (Ithaca: Cornell University Press, 1981) 418-25.

[76]Troeltsch, *The Social Teachings of the Christian Churches*, 1:85-86.

attitude was not founded on love and esteem for the existing institutions, but upon a mixture of contempt, submission, and relative recognition. That is why, in spite of all submissiveness, Christianity did destroy the Roman state by alienating souls from its ideals, and it has a disintegrating effect upon all undiluted nationalism and upon every form of exclusively earthly authority.[77]

"Paulinism," according to Troeltsch, recognized and accommodated itself to social phenomena—institutions and organizations—"mingled with a spirit of inner detachment and independence." "This . . . suggested a positive relationship which was capable of further development and one which . . . later, was increasingly produced by the early church. But . . . this attitude never became a programme of social reform, nor even possibly of a Christian civilization."[78] In fact, most of the New Testament stands out in terms of its lack of attention to social and political problems, as Günther Bornkamm has made very clear.

> Nowhere in the New Testament outside the Revelation of John do we find scorn and hostility against the empire as they were known in the gloomy political predictions of the so-called Sibylline Oracles and in the threatening prophecy of late Jewish apocalyptic from the East, and also on Roman soil in the latter period of the Republic and in the time of the emperors. Nowhere do we hear anything of the voices of oppressed peoples, who gave vent to their rebellion against Rome's rapacity and unsatisfiable destructive fury in the manner of the King of Britain in Tacitus (*Agric.* 30). Nowhere do we hear the voice of loathing with which the educated Greeks scorned the cultureless, snobbish, and noisy activity of Rome, nor the voice of painful boredom with which Rome's own writers and poets now and then in the time of the civil war weighed and recommended to the prudent the surrender of the capital city and the flight to the country or even to the blessed stillness of distant islands.[79]

---

[77]Ibid., 82.

[78]Ibid., 83-84.

[79]Günther Bornkamm, "Christ and the World in the Early Christian Message," in his *Early Christian Experience,* Paul L. Hammer, trans. (New York: Harper & Row Publishers, 1969) 20-21. John Armstrong, *The Idea of Holiness and the Humane Response* (London: George Allen & Unwin, 1981) 99-128, in his discussion of holiness and the humane response in the age of the Fathers, is in complete agreement with Bornkamm. See also L. William Countryman, *The Rich Christian in the Church of the Early Empire* (New York and Toronto: The Edwin Mellen Press, 1980) ch. 2 and the conclusion, for discussion about early Christian attitude towards wealth as attitude towards society.

The reason most of the New Testament writers (including Paul) did not address the world in social and political criticism in the manner in which other writers in the Greco-Roman world did,[80] was due to the construction of a different "world," or symbolic universe in response to the world as it presented itself in all its sociopolitical aspects.[81]

Although Rudolf Bultmann generally tends towards overinterpretation in an attempt to fit it into his overall theological system, in an essay entitled "The Understanding of Man and the World in the New Testament and in the Greek World,"[82] his explication of 1 Corinthians 7:29-31 is not without poignancy. The passage, he says, represents "eschatological reservation,"[83] not involving an "either/or" with respect of Greece—the world—and faith. "[T]he question of Greece or Christianity is one which always confronts man." Paul recognized that the world was the sphere of Christian existence and obedience, that he had "need of Greece for his action in the world."[84] The important question was the "significance of his activity." Because the world is thought not to have the same receptivity to God's commands, and because it tends to frustrate the efforts of those whose concern is to respond to those commands, Christian existence must be a "continual limitation" of the world, a "taking out" of the world, "as a means of adequately expressing eschatological existence in the given world

---

[80]See Harold Fuchs's *Der Geistige Widerstand Gegen Rom in der Antiken Welt* (Berlin: Walter De Gruyter & Co., 1938) for references.

[81]Cf. Hock, *The Social Context of Paul's Ministry*, 81; D. Kienast, "Ein vernachlässigtes Zeugnis für die Reichpolitik Trajans: Die zweits tarsische Rede des Dion von Prusa," *Historia* 20 (1971): 62-80; Glen W. Bowersock, *Augustus and the Greek World* (Oxford: Clarendon Press, 1965) 85-100; Kautsky, *The Politics of Aristocratic Empires,* 320-38. Hock, following Bowersock and Kienast, makes the point that in the eastern Empire under Augustus political power and responsibility lay in the hands of provincial authorities. Their whims made social protest a precarious venture for all but the most respected and powerful citizens (cf. Hock, 91n198). Kautsky, as I have already mentioned, argues that the townspeople of all aristocratic empires were and are generally powerless, without any hope of significant structural change in their interest and improvement. Only the dawn of commercialization—the development of technology and nonaristocratic markets—realized significant changes for *opportunities* for structural changes and protest (cf. Kautsky, 336).

[82]In his *Essays: Philosophical and Theological*, James C. G. Grieg, trans. (London: SCM Press, 1958) 67-89.

[83]Ibid., 86.

[84]Ibid., 87.

situation.''[85] This made the world free for engagement, since the renunciation is never simply reaction to a state of affairs prevailing within the world, but a response to concern about ''the things of the Lord.''

Sociologist Robert A. Nisbet[86] echoes Bultmann's and Troeltsch's general sentiments. But in his discussion regarding early Christianity's role in terms of the history of community building and social conflict in the West, Nisbet goes beyond them in seeing the impact of the early Christians below the level of the headlines. Since early Christianity's *redefinition* and *restructuring* of kinship ties represented a radical allegiance, encompassing the totality of life, it affected the most serious (though subtle) challenge to the Empire. In effect, it took the ''heart'' out of the Empire not only in its radical allegiance to another power, but also in its creation of whole new basic units of social existence—the Christian οἶκος.

Again, this means that those Christians were less indifferent to the world in which they lived than they were critical of it through their religious experience, namely, in a way consonant with their self-understanding and position in the sociopolitical context.

The Pauline Christians came to reject the ways of cultic markers or separatism and pneumatic-elitist renunciation as models of spirituality (social orientation). The former they rejected because their communities were to be open to all, irrespective of ethnic-religious origins, the latter because the ''things of the world'' are in the final analysis not evil, not to be renounced, only to be relativized and reprioritized under the concern for the ''things of the Lord.''

It should not at all be surprising that Paul, as a leader of the fledgling Christian community in Corinth, and as one with high-status achievement and low-status attribution, should counsel a more ''worldly,'' domesticated model of ascetic behavior of the type associated with the elite classes of outsiders.[87] Such counseling betrays *missionary* impulses broadly defined—to commend himself, his fledgling communities and their message to the established circles of the Empire. Such an interest is perhaps the perennial preoccupation of those in the ''middle.''

---

[85]Ibid., 88.

[86]See his *The Social Philosophers: Community and Conflict in Western Thought* (New York: Thomas Y. Crowell, Inc., 1973) 174-81.

[87]Cf. Theissen, *The Social Setting of Pauline Christianity,* My more limited, focused argument relative to the passage examined squares with Theissen's general arguments about Paul and the ''strong'' among the Corinthians (cf. 121-44).

Summary Conclusion

The findings of our study may be summarized as follows.

1. ῾Ως μή reflects, it does not determine, the social orientation and self-understanding of a significant segment of early Christianity—the urban Pauline mission. This social orientation and self-understanding are evident from the language (in addition to ὡς μή) that the Pauline Christians used, from their rituals, and, most clearly, in the *pattern* of their engagement of practical social issues.

2. The ὡς μή exhortations express the pattern of *ambivalence* or *tension* in the Pauline Christians' response to the urban Greco-Roman world. The ὡς μή passage is significant not only because its larger context is itself one *case-example* of the pattern of the Pauline Christians' response to the urban Greco-Roman world, but also because it provides one of the rare early Christian self-conscious reflections on Christian existence, its structure and implications. It opens a window into some of the influential factors (e.g., social status, social status inclinations, structure of sociopolitical order, and social setting) that constituted the model and understanding of Christian existence for Paul and the Pauline mission.

3. The ὡς μή passage indicates that Christian existence was *assumed* by the Pauline Christians (no doubt, also by other early Christian "denominations") to entail a mode of ascetic behavior, a form of renunciation. The expectation of the parousia, it is made clear, was not the abstract dogmatic precipitant for this assumption; this expectation was itself a *reflection* of assumptions about the new existence in Christ. It was rather the particular "form" or "model" of renunciation that was at issue. Paul was faced with questions about the life-style of married Christians, Christians involved in mixed marriages, singles considering marriage, widows considering remarriage—in short, about the nature of Christian existence. He had received an inquiry in writing. He knows and openly admits that most of the questions asked are new questions for which he has no command from the

Lord. Hence, he gives his advice, concluding with an ironic note—δοκῶ δὲ κἀγὼ πνεῦμα θεοῦ ἔχειν (v. 40b).

In the process of giving advice, Paul gives his critique of the attitude and views he perceives on the part of the Corinthians. In many respects he shares their sentiments, but he is reluctant to make their rigorous ascetic inclinations and views hard and binding rules for all. Those who cannot follow the rigorous standards of asceticism do not sin. And it is important that the "strong" understand this view.

It is in grappling with this pastoral problem that Paul hits upon and makes use of stereotyped prophetic-eschatological speech. This he uses, among other arguments, toward the *relativizing* of the rigoristic views of some of the Corinthians. *Thus, the relativizing argument ((ὡς μή = ἀμέριμνος) is used not for debunking, but for accepting involvement in, the structures of the world, with the proviso that concern for "the things of the Lord" take priority.*

What seems to have inspired Paul's model of ascetic behavior was his concern that unity, edification, propriety, good order and missions not be frustrated. As far as he was concerned, the goal for the churches of his mission should be the realization of a *quality* of human relationships. The "worldly" perspective, not "flight from the world" into ecstasy or enthusiasm, inspires and facilitates the ethical shaping of human relationships. That Paul and his churches did not revolutionize the shape of social relationships in the larger world of which they were a part is clear enough. This was due to many factors, not the least of which was the character of that (socioeconomic-political) world and their (socioeconomic-political) place in it. That many could and would interpret their perspective as legitimation of a social conservatism that would function to frustrate egalitarian aspirations is, sadly, history, but is due to a confusion of the force of the issues in the original context of debate and discussion.[1] Again, for Paul and for most of his churches, the central concern seems to have been the quality of social relationships in the churches. Radical renunciation, to the extent that it was associated with spiritual solipsism, compromised this

---

[1]See Elisabeth Schüssler Fiorenza's *In Memory of Her: A Feminist Theological Reconstruction of Christian Origins* (New York: Crossroad, 1983) 205-334, and *Bread Not Stone: The Challenge of Feminist Biblical Interpretation* (Boston: Beacon Press, 1985) 65-92, for examples of critical discussion which I think is built on defensible understanding of the original force of the issues raised.

concern, and so was rejected. What was embraced was a *midddle-of-the-road* approach, a "worldly asceticism," spiritual and psychological detachment. Such approach on the part of those for the most part variously situated in the "middle" of their social world should occasion no surprise.

Our contribution has been to help establish more clearly (Paul and) the Pauline churches not as a withdrawn "sect" indifferent to the world around them, but as fledgling communities *experimenting* with a new mode of existence in the world, struggling to discover what concern for "the things of the Lord" must mean in the world they knew.

The "first urban Christians" sized up the world in which they lived, the options it afforded them, and in general opted for a "worldly" model of existence that allowed them freedom to "use" the world in pursuit of "the things of the Lord." Their experiences provide no security for those who *in their name* would register piety in otherworldliness or ecstasy.

The struggles of Paul and the Pauline Christians to concern themselves with "the things of the Lord" in the world as a *middle-of-the-road* ethic remains both as baggage and challenge for every subsequent model of Christian spirituality. For those for whom Christian faith demands and is synonymous with a worldly agenda for aggressive social change, the way of Paul and the Pauline Christians will appear embarrassingly weak and irrelevant. For those for whom Christian faith demands the development of interior piety first and foremost, the way of Paul and the Pauline Christians will appear to be substandard, a worldly compromise.

But the struggles of Paul and the Pauline Christians—and the dialogue that chronicles such struggles—will remain a challenge for every subsequent model of Christian spirituality: not to dictate the shape of the model for all generations and in every cultural context, but to demonstrate the freedom with which the pursuit of "the things of the Lord" in the world can be joined and made meaningful in different ways not only for each new generation, but also for each cultural context and individual. So the real lesson to be learned from the discussion between Paul and some of the Corinthians is not in the middle-of-the-road, socially conservative ethic, but in the fact that not even this advice is to be absolutized, since personal endowment and situation are said to determine its relevance. This is the challenge of ὡς μή. It may be safe to say that neither category of detractors—worldly/social activists, enthusiasts—in Western Christendom up to the modern era has risen to this challenge.

It is hoped that the attempt to analyze the origin and function of this very suggestive passage will establish a new baseline for its future use not alone in studies in the history and diversification of early Christianity, but also in efforts to understand more clearly the religious heritage of the West. Perhaps, such clarity can help efforts to reshape this heritage to meet present and future challenges and yearnings.

Bibliography

Primary Texts and Tools

Aeschylus. Translated by Herbert Weir Smyth. Two volumes. Loeb Classical Library. New York: G. P. Putnam's Sons, 1926.

The Ante-Nicene Fathers. Translations of the Writings of the Fathers down to A.D. 325. Edited by Alexander Roberts and James Donaldson; American edition edited by A. Cleveland Coxe. Ten volumes. Grand Rapids MI: Wm. B. Eerdmans Publishing Company, 1885-1886; reprint, 1981.

Apostolic Fathers. Translated by Kirsopp Lake. Loeb Classical Library. Two volumes. Cambridge MA: Harvard University Press, 1914; reprint, 1977.

Aristotle. *The Nichomachean Ethics*. Translated by H. Rackham. Loeb Classical Library. Cambridge MA: Harvard University Press, 1926; reprint, 1945.

Bauer, Walter. *A Greek-English Lexicon of the New Testament and Other Early Christian Literature*. Translated and edited by William F. Arndt and F. Wilbur Gingrich. Chicago: University of Chicago Press, 1957.

Biblia Patristica: Index des Citations et Allusions Bibliques dans la Littérature Patristique. Paris: Université des science humaines de Strasbourg. Centre d'Analyse et de documentation patristiques, 1975.

Blass, Friedrich, and Albert Debrunner. *A Greek Grammar of the New Testament and Other Early Christian Literature*. Translated and revised by Robert W. Funk. Chicago: University of Chicago Press, 1961. Citations by section.

Calvin, John. *Commentary on the Epistles of Paul the Apostle to the Corinthians*. Calvin's Commentaries 20. Translated by John Pringle. Edited by John King, et al. Grand Rapids: Baker Book House, 1981.

Charlesworth, John Hamilton, ed. *Old Testament Pseudepigrapha*. Volume 1. Garden City: Doubleday, 1983.

Cramer, J. A., ed. *Catenae graecorum patrum*. Five volumes. Oxford: Oxford University Press, 1844.

Dio Chrysostom. *Discourses*. Translated by J. W. Cohoon. Loeb Classical Library. Five volumes. Cambridge MA: Harvard University Press, 1939; reprint, 1977.

Epictetus. *The Discourses as Reported by Arrian, the Manual and Fragments*. Translated by W. A. Oldfather. Two volumes. Loeb Classical Library. Cambridge MA: Harvard University Press, 1928; reprint, 1978.

Eusebius. *The Ecclesiastical History*. Translated by Kirsopp Lake. Volume 7. Cambridge MA: Harvard University Press, 1926.

Foerster, Werner, ed. *Gnosis*. Translated by R. McL. Wilson. Two volumes. Oxford: Oxford University Press, 1972.

Fritzsche, Otto, ed. *Libri Apocryphi Veteris Testamenti Graece*. Recensuit et cum commentario critico. Accedunt libri Veteris Testamenti pseydepigraphi selecti. Lipsiae: Brockhaus, 1871.

Grimm, Carl Ludwig Wilibald. *A Greek-English Lexicon of the New Testament*. Translated, revised, and enlarged by Joseph Henry Thayer. 4th ed. Edinburg: T. & T. Clark, 1901.

Hastings, James, ed. "Asceticism." *Encyclopedia of Religion and Ethics*. Volume 2. Edinburgh: T & T Clark, 1909.

Hatch, Edwin, and H. A. Redpath. *A Concordance to the Septuagint and Other Greek Versions of the Old Testament*. Two volumes. Graz, Austria: Akademische Druck-und Verlaganstalt, 1897; 1954.

Hennecke, Edgar, ed. *New Testament Apocrypha*. New edition edited by William Schneemelcher. English Translation edited by R. McL. Wilson. Two volumes. Philadelphia: Westminster Press, 1963.

Herodotus. Translated by Alfred D. Godley. Loeb Classical Library. Four volumes. Cambridge MA: Harvard University Press, 1956.

Irenaeus. *Against Heresies*. In *The Ante-Nicene Fathers*, 7:315-567. Edited by Rev. Alexander Roberts and James Donaldson. Revised by A. Cleveland Coxe. Reprint, 1981.

Kittel, Gerhard, and Gerhard Friedrich, eds. *Theological Dictionary of the New Testament*. Translated by Geoffrey W. Bromiley. Nine volumes. Grand Rapids MI: Wm. B. Eerdmans Publishing Company, 1964-1974.

Liddell, Henry G., and Robert Scott. *A Greek-English Lexicon*. Revised and augmented by H. S. Jones and R. McKenzie. Oxford: Clarendon Press, 1968; reprint, 1978.

Luther, Martin. "The Christian in Society III." In *Luther's Works*. Various Translators. Edited by R. C. Schutz. American Edition. Philadelphia: Fortress Press, 1967.

Luther, Martin. "Commentary on 1 Corinthians 7." Volume 28, pages 3-56, of *Luther's Works*. Translated by Edward Sitter. Edited by Hilton C. Oswald. American Edition. St. Louis: Concordia Publishing House, 1973.

Menander. Translated by F. G. Allinson. Loeb Classical Library. Cambridge MA: Harvard University Press, 1964.

Moulton, William F., and Alfred S. Geden. *A Concordance to the Greek Testament*. Fifth edition revised by Harold K. Moulton. Edinburgh: T. & T. Clark, 1978.

Nestle, Eberhard, Kurt Aland, et al., eds. *Novum Testamentum Graece*. Twenty-sixth edition. Stuttgart: Deutsche Bibelgesellschaft, 1979.

Oates, Whitney J., ed. *The Stoic and Epicurean Philosophers. The Complete Writings of Epicurus, Epictetus, Lucretius, Marcus Aurelius*. New York: Random House, 1940.

Philo. *Works*. Translated by F. H. Colson, G. H. Whitaker, and R. Marcus. Loeb Classical Library. Twelve volumes. Cambridge MA: Harvard University Press, 1934-1961.

Pindar. Translated by John Sandys. Loeb Classical Library. New York: G. P. Putnam's Sons, 1927.

Plato. *The Collected Dialogues, including the Letters*. Edited by Edith Hamilton and Huntington Cairns. Bollingen Series 71. Princeton NJ: Princeton University Press, 1961.

Plotinus. Translated by A. H. Armstrong. Loeb Classical Library. Three volumes. Cambridge MA: Harvard University Press, 1966.

Porphyry. *Vita Plotinus*. Translated by A. H. Armstrong. Loeb Classical Library. Cambridge MA: Harvard University Press, 1966.

Pseudo-Aristotle. *De Mundo*. Translated by D. J. Furley. Loeb Classical Library. Cambridge MA: Harvard University Press, 1955.

Robinson, James M., ed. *The Nag Hammadi Library in English*. Leiden: E. J. Brill, 1977.

Seneca. *De Brevitate Vitae. De Ira. De Consolatione ad Marciam*. Translated by John W. Basore. Loeb Classical Library. Cambridge MA: Harvard University Press, 1932; reprint, 1979.

_____. *Naturales Quaestiones*. Translated by T. H. Corcoran. Loeb Classical Library. Two volumes. Cambridge MA: Harvard University Press, 1971.

_____. Epistulae Morales. Translated by R. M. Gummere. Loeb Classical Library. Three volumes. Cambridge MA: Harvard University Press, 1917-1925.

Sextus Empiricus. Translated by R. G. Bury. Loeb Classical Library. Four volumes. Cambridge MA: Harvard University Press, 1955.

Sophocles. Translated by Francis Storr. Loeb Classical Library. Two volumes. Cambridge MA: Harvard University Press, 1951.

Staab, Karl, ed. *Pauluskommentare aus der griechischen Kirche aus Katenenhandschriften*. Neutestamentliche Abhandlungen 15. Münster: Aschendorff, 1933.

Stobaeus. *Florilegium*. Edited by Augustus Meineke. Four volumes. Leipzig: B.-G. Teubner, 1855-1867.

[Strack, Hermann L., and] Paul Billerbeck. *Kommentar zum Neuen Testament aus Talmud und Midrash*. Four volumes. Munchen: C. H. Beck'sche Verlagsbuchhandlung, 1922-1928.

Thucydides. Translated by Charles F. Smith. Loeb Classical Library. Four volumes. New York: G. P. Putnam's Sons, 1931.

von Arnim, H. *Stoicum Veterum Fragmenta*. Four volumes. Leipzig: 1903-1924; reprint, Stuttgart, 1964.

Xenophon. *Cyropaedia*. Translated by Walter Miller. Loeb Classical Library. Two volumes. New York: G. P. Putnam's Sons, 1925

_____. *Memorabilia and Oeconomicus*. Translated by E. C. Marchant. Loeb Classical Library. New York: G. P. Putnam's Sons, 1923.

Secondary Sources

Armstrong, John. *The Idea of Holiness and the Humane Response: A Study of the Concept of Holiness and Its Social Consequences*. London: George Allen & Unwin, 1981.

Aune, David. *Prophecy in Early Christianity*. Grand Rapids MI: Eerdmans Publishing Co., 1983.

Bach, Robert. *Die Aufforderung zur Flucht und zum Kampf im Alttestamentlichen Prophetenspruch*. WMANT 9. Neukirchener Verlag, 1962.

Baird, William. "Pauline Eschatology in Hermeneutical Perspective." *NTS* 17 (1971): 314-27.

Balch, David. "Backgrounds of 1 Cor. 7." *NTS* 18 (1971): 351-64.

_____. "1 Cor. 7:32-35, Marriage, Anxiety and Distraction." *JBL* 102,3 (1983): 429-39.

Baltensweiler, Heinrich. *Die Ehe im Neuen Testament: Exegetische Untersuchungen über Ehe, Ehelosigkeit und Ehescheidung.* Abhandlungen zur Theologie des Alten und Neuen Testaments 52. Stuttgart: Zwingli Verlag, 1967.

Barrett, C. K. *The First Epistle to the Corinthians.* Harpers New Testament Commentaries. New York and Evanston: Harper & Row Publishers, 1968.

Bartchy, S. Scott. *Mallon Chresai: First Century Slavery and the Interpretation of 1 Cor. 7:21.* Society of Biblical Literature Dissertation Series 11. Missoula MT: Scholars Press, 1973.

Bauer, Bruno. *Christus und die Caesaren: Der Ursprung des Christentums aus dem römischen Griechentum.* Hildescheim: Olms, 1877; reprint, 1879.

Baumgarten, Jörg. *Paulus und die Apokalyptik: Die Auslegung apokalyptischer Uberlieferungen in den echten Paulusbriefen.* Wissenschaftliche Monographien zum Alten und Neuen Testament 44. Neukirchen: Neukirchener Verlag, 1975.

Becker, Jürgen. "Erwängungen zur apokalyptischen Tradition in der paulinischen Theologie." *EvTh* 30 (1970): 593-609.

Beker, J. Christiaan. *Paul the Apostle: The Triumph of God in Life and Thought.* Philadelphia: Fortress Press, 1980.

_____. *Paul's Apocalyptic Gospel.* Philadelphia: Fortress Press, 1982.

Bellah, Robert N. "Religious Evolution." Pages 36-50 in *Reader in Comparative Religion: An Anthropological Approach.* Third edition. Edited by William A. Lessa and Evon Z. Vogt. New York: Harper & Row Publishers, 1972.

Bertram, Georg. καλός. *TDNT* 3 (1965) 536-56.

Betz, Hans Dieter. "On the Problem of the Religio-Historical Understanding of Apocalypticism." *JTC* 6:134-56. Edited by Robert W. Funk. New York: Herder and Herder, 1969.

Bjerkelund, Carl J. *Parakalō: Form, Funktion, und Sinn der parakolō-Sätze in den paulinischen Briefen.* Bibliotheca Theologica Norwegica Oslo: Universitetsforlaget, 1967.

Bonhöffer, Adolf. *Epiktet und das Neue Testament.* Religionsgeschichtliche Versuche und Vorarbeiten 10. Giessen: Alfred Töpelmann Verlag, 1911.

Bornkamm, Günther. "Christ and the World in the Early Christian Message." Pages 14-28 in his *Early Christian Experience.* Translated by Paul L. Hammer. New York: Harper & Row, Publishers, 1969.

_____. *Paul.* Translated by D. M. G. Stalker. New York: Harper & Row Publishers, 1971.

Bowersock, Glen W. *Augustus and the Greek World.* Oxford: Clarendon Press, 1965.

Braun, Herbert. "Die Indifferenz gegenüber der Welt bei Paulus und bei Epiktet." In his *Gesammelte Studien zum Neuen Testament und Seiner Umwelt.* Second edition. Tübingen: J. C. B. Mohr (Paul Siebeck), 1967. 159-67.

Brown, Peter. *The Making of Late Antiquity.* Cambridge MA: Harvard University Press, 1971.

_____. "The Philosopher and Society in Late Antiquity." Pages 1-17 in *Protocol of the Thirty-Fourth Colloquy of the Center for Hermeneutical Studies.* Edited by Edward C. Hobbs and Wilhelm Wuellner. Berkeley CA: The Center for Hermeneutical Studies in Hellenistic and Modern Culture, 1980.

_____. "The Rise and Function of the Holy Man in Late Antiquity." *JRomSt* (1971): 80-101.

Bultmann, Rudolf. ἀμέριμνος. *TDNT* 4 (1967) 593.

_____. *Existence and Faith*. Edited and translated by Schubert Ogden. New York: The World Publishing Company, 1961.

_____. *Glauben und Verstehen: Gesammelte Aufsätze*. I, II, III, IV. Tübingen: J. C. B. Mohr (Paul Siebeck) 1933, 1952, 1960, 1965.

_____, et al. *Kerygma and Myth: A Theological Debate*. Edited by Hans Werner Bartsch. Revised translation by Reginald H. Fuller. New York: Harper & Row, 1961.

_____. *Primitive Christianity in its Contemporary Setting*. Translated by Reginald H. Fuller. Cleveland and New York: World/Meridian Press, 1956.

_____. *Theology of the New Testament*. Translated by Kendrick Grobel. Two volumes. New York: Scribners, 1951, 1955.

_____. "The Understanding of World and Man in the New Testament and in the Greek World." Pages 67-89 in his *Essays: Philosophical and Theological*. Translated by James C. G. Grieg. London: SCM Press, 1958. German original: "Das Verständnis von Welt und Mensch im Neuen Testament und im Griechentum." Pages 59-78 in *Glauben und Verstehen* II (1952).

Cadoux C. J. "The Imperatival Use of ἵνα in the New Testament." *JTS* 42 (1941): 165-73.

Campenhausen, Hans von. "The Christian and Social Life." Pages 141-59 in his *Tradition and Life in the Church. Essays and Lectures in Church History*. Philadelphia: Fortress Press, 1968.

Cartlidge, David. "Competing Theologies in Early Christian Asceticism." Th.D. dissertation, Harvard University, 1969.

Collins, John J. "Chiasmus, the 'ABA' Pattern and the Text of Paul." Pages 575-84 in *Studiorum Paulinorum Congressus Internationalis Catholicus*. Analecta Biblica 17. Rome: Biblical Institute Press, 1963.

Conzelmann, Hans. *1 Corinthians: A Commentary on the First Epistle to the Corinthians*. Translated by James W. Leitch. Bibliography and references by James W. Dunkly. Edited by George W. MacRae. Philadelphia: Fortress Press, 1975.

Countryman, L. William. *The Rich Christian in the Church of the Early Empire: Contradictions and Accommodations*. New York and Toronto: The Edwin Mellen Press, 1980.

Cullmann, Oscar. *Christ and Time: The Primitive Christian Conception of Time and History*. Translated by Floyd V. Filson. Philadelphia: Westminster Press, 1950.

_____. *Salvation in History*. Translated by Sidney G. Sowers and SCM Press Ltd., London. First American Edition. New York: Harper & Row Publishers, 1967.

Dahl, Nils A. "Paul and the Church at Corinth According to 1 Cor. 1:10-4:21." Pages 40-61 in his *Studies in Paul: Theology for the Early Christian Mission*. Minneapolis: Augsburg Press, 1977.

_____. "The One God of Jews and Gentiles." Pages 178-91 in his *Studies in Paul: Theology for the Early Christian Mission*. Minneapolis: Augsburg Press, 1977.

Delling, Gerhard. καιρός. *TDNT* 3 (1965) 455-64.

Dieckman, Bernard. *"Welt und Entweltlichung" in der Theologie Rudolf Bultmanns: Zum Zusammenshang von Welt- und Heilsverständnis*. Beiträge zur Ökumenischen Theologie 17. Munich: Verlag Ferdinand Schöningh, 1977.

Dinkler, Erich. "Zum Problem der Ethik bei Paulus." *ZThK* 49 (1952): 167-200.

Dodds, E. R. *Pagan and Christian in an Age of Anxiety: Some Aspects of Religious Experience from Marcus Aurelius to Constantine*. New York: W. W. Norton and Company, 1965.

Doughty, Darrell. "Heiligkeit und Freiheit: Eine exegetische Untersuchung der Anwendung des paulinischen Freiheitsgedankens in 1 Kor 7." Ph.D. dissertation, Göttingen University, 1965.

_____. "History and Eschatology in the Theology of Paul: An Outline of the Present Discussion." *The Drew Gateway* 42,3 (1972): 168-87.

_____. "The Presence and Future of Salvation in Corinth." *ZNW* 66 (1975): 61-90.

Douglas, Mary. *Natural Symbols: Explorations in Cosmology*. Second edition. London: Barrie & Jenkins, 1973.

_____. *Purity and Danger*. London: Routledge & Kegan Paul, 1966.

Dungan, David L. *The Sayings of Jesus in the Churches of Paul: The Use of the Synoptic Tradition in the Regulation of Early Church Life*. Philadelphia: Fortress Press, 1971.

Dunn, James D. G. *Jesus and the Spirit: A Study of the Religious and Charismatic Experience of Jesus and the First Christians as Reflected in the New Testament*. Philadelphia: Westminster, 1975.

_____. *Unity and Diversity in the New Testament: An Inquiry into the Character of Earliest Christianity*. Philadelphia: Westminster, 1977.

Durkheim, Emile. *The Elementary Forms of the Religious Life*. Translated by J. W. Swain, 1915. Reprint: New York: Free Press, 1965.

Edelstein, Ludwig. *The Meaning of Stoicism*. Cambridge MA: Harvard University Press, 1966.

Elliott, John H. *A Home for the Homeless: A Sociological Exegesis of 1 Peter, Its Situation and Strategy*. Philadelphia: Fortress, 1981.

Enslin, Morton S. *The Ethics of Paul*. New York: Harper & Brothers Publishers, 1930.

Festguière, Andre-Jean. *Personal Religion among the Greeks*. Second edition. Berkeley: University of California Press, 1960.

Fiorenza, Elisabeth Schüssler. *In Memory of Her: A Feminist Theological Reconstruction of Christian Origins*. New York: Crossroad, 1983.

_____. *Bread Not Stone: The Challenge of Feminist Biblical Interpretation*. Boston: Beacon Press, 1985.

Fleury, A. *Saint Paul et Sénèque, Reserches sur les rapports du philosophe avec l'apotre sur l'infiltration du christianisme naissant a travers le paganisme*. Two volumes. Paris: Ladrange, 1853.

Freedman, David Noel. "The Flowering of Apocalyptic." *JThC* 6:166-74. Edited by Robert W. Funk. New York: Herder and Herder, 1969.

Frotzheim, Franzjosef. *Christologie und Eschatologie bei Paulus*. Forschung zur Bibel 35. Gesamtherstellung: Echter Verlag, 1979.

Fuchs, Harald. *Der Geistige Widerstand gegen Rom in der Antiken Welt*. Berlin: Walter De Gruyter & Co., 1938.

Gager, John. "Functional Diversity in Paul's Use of End-Time Language." *JBL* 89 (1970): 325-37.

Glasswell, M. E. "Some Issues of Church and Society in the Light of Paul's Eschatology." Pages 310-19 in *Paul and Paulinism. Essays in Honour of C. K. Barrett*. Edited by M. D. Hooker and S. G. Wilson. London: SPCK, 1982.

Grant, Frederick C., ed. *Hellenistic Religions: The Age of Syncretism*. Indianapolis: Bobbs-Merrill Company, 1953.

Grant, Robert M. *Early Christianity and Society: Seven Studies*. San Francisco: Harper and Row Publishers, 1977.

Greeven, Heinrich. *Das Hauptproblem der Sozialethik in der neueren Stoa und im Urchristentum*. Neutestamentliche Forschungen 4. Gütersloh: Verlag C. Bertelsmann, 1935.

Gundry, Robert H. *SŌMA in Biblical Theology, with Emphasis on Pauline Anthropology*. Cambridge: Cambridge University Press, 1976.

Hierzenberger, Gottfried. *Weltbewertung bei Paulus nach 1 Kor 7, 29-31. Eine exegetisch-Kerygmatische Studie*. Düsseldorf: Patmos-Verlag, 1967.

Hobbs, Edward C., and Wilhelm Wuellner, eds. *Protocol of the Thirty-Fourth Colloquy of the Center for Hermeneutical Studies*. Berkeley: The Center for Hermeneutical Studies in Hellenistic and Modern Culture, 1980.

Hock, Ronald. *The Social Context of Paul's Ministry: Tentmaking and Apostleship*. Philadelphia: Fortress, 1980.

Holmberg, Bengt. *Paul and Power: The Structure of Authority in the Primitive Church as Reflected in the Pauline Epistles*. Philadelphia: Fortress, 1980.

Hooker, M. D. and S. G. Wilson, eds. *Paul and Paulinism: Essays in Honour of C. K. Barrett*. London: SPCK, 1982.

Hurd, John Coolidge, Jr. *The Origin of 1 Corinthians*. Corrected reprint: Macon GA: Mercer University Press, 1983.

Jensen, Joseph. "Does Porneia Mean Fornication?" *NovTest* 20 (1978): 161-84.

Jonas, Hans. *Gnosis und Spätantiker Geist*. Volume 2, part 1. Göttingen: Vandenhoeck & Ruprecht, 1966.

_____. *The Gnostic Religion: The Message of the Alien God and the Beginnings of Christianity*. Second revised edition. Boston: Beacon Press, 1962.

Judge, E. A. " 'Antike und Christentum': Towards a Definition of the Field. A Bibliographic Survey." Pages 3-58 in *Aufstieg und Niedergang der römischen Welt*. II.23.1. Edited by Hildegard Temporini and Wolfgang Haase. Berlin and New York: Walter De Gruyter, 1979.

Käsemann, Ernst. "The Beginnings of Christian Theology." *JTC* 6:17-46. Edited by Robert W. Funk. New York: Herder and Herder, 1969.

_____. "On the Subject of Primitive Christian Apocalyptic." In his *New Testament Questions of Today*. Translated by W. J. Montague and Wilfred F. Bunge. Philadelphia: Fortress Press, 1969.

Kautzky, John H. *The Politics of Aristocratic Empires*. Chapel Hill: University of North Carolina Press, 1982.

Kidd, I. G. "Moral Actions and Rules in Stoic Ethics." Pages 247-58 in *The Stoics*. Edited by John M. Rist. Berkeley: University of California, 1978.

Kienast, D. "Ein vernachlässigtes Zeugnis fur die Reichpolitik Trajans: Die zweits tarsische Rede des Dion von Prusa," *Historia* 20 (1971): 62-80.

Klein, Günther. "Apokalyptische Naherwartung bei Paulus." Pages 241-62 in *Neues Testament und christliche Existenz. Festschrift für Herbert Braun.* Edited by H. D. Betz and Luise Schottroff. Tübingen: J. C. B. Mohr (Paul Siebeck), 1973.

Koch, Klaus. *The Rediscovery of Apocalyptic: A Polemical Work on a Neglected Area of Biblical Studies and its Damaging Effects on Theology and Philosophy.* Naperville IL: A. R. Allenson, 1972.

Kümmel, Werner. "Verlobung und Heirat bei Paulus (1 Kor 7, 36-38)." Pages 310-27 in his *Heilsgeschehen und Geschichte: Gesammelte Aufsätze 1933-1964.* Edited by Erich Grässer, Otto Merk, and Adolf Fritz. Marburg: N. G. Elwert Verlag, 1965.

Kuiper, K. *Epictetus en de christelijke moraal.* Verslagen en Medeelingen Der K. Akad. van Wetenschappen. Afd. Letterkunde. Amsterdam, 1906.

Lapidus, Ira M. "Response, to Peter Brown." Pages 25-26 in *Protocol of the Thirty-Fourth Colloquy of the Center for Hermeneutical Studies.* Edited by Edward C. Hobbs and Wilhelm Weullner. Berkeley: Center for Hermeneutical Studies, 1980.

Laub, Franz. *Eschatologie, Verkündigung und Lebensgestaltung nach Paulus: Eine Untersuchhung zum Wirken des Apostels beim Aufbau der Gemeinde in Thessalonike.* Biblische Untersuchugen Herausgegeben von Otto Kuss 10. Regensburg: Verlag Friedrich Pustet, 1973.

Lebram, J. C. H. "The Piety of the Jewish Apocalyptists." In *Apocalypticism in the Mediterranean World and the Near East.* Edited by D. Hellholm. Tübingen: J. C. B. Mohr (Paul Siebeck), 1983.

Lessa, W. A. and Vogt, E. Z., eds. *Reader in Comparative Religion.* Third edition. New York: Harper and Row Publishers, 1972.

Lietzmann, Hans. *Eschatologie, Verkündigung und Lebengestaltung nach Paulus: Eine Untersuchung zum Wirken des Apostels beim Aufbau der Gemeinde in Thessalonike.* Biblische Untersuchungen Herausgegeben von Otto Kuss 10. Regensburg: Verlag Friedrich Pustet, 1973.

_____. *An die Korinther 1, 2.* HNT 9. Second edition. Tübingen: J. C. B. Mohr (Paul Siebeck) 1949.

Lincoln, Andrew T. *Paradise Now and Not Yet: Studies in the Role of the Heavenly Dimension in Paul's Thought with Reference to his Eschatology.* Cambridge: Cambridge University Press, 1981.

Lindemann, Andreas. *Paulus im ältesten Christentum: das Bild des Apostels und die Rezeption der paulinischen Theologie in der frühchristlichen Literatur bis Marcion.* Tübingen: J. C. B. Mohr (Paul Siebeck), 1979.

Lohse, Bernhard. *Askese und Mönchtum in der Antike und in der alten Kirche.* München: R. Oldenburg, 1969.

MacDonald, Dennis Ronald. *The Legend and the Apostle: The Battle for Paul in Story and Canon.* Philadelphia: Westminster Press, 1983.

MacMullen, Ramsay. *Enemies of the Roman Order: Treason, Unrest, and Alienation in the Empire.* Cambridge MA: Harvard University Press, 1966.

_____. *Paganism in the Roman Empire.* New Haven and London: Yale University Press, 1981.

MacRae, George W. "Why the Church Rejected Gnosticism." Pages 126-33 in *Jewish and Christian Self-Definition.* Edited by E. P. Sanders. Philadelphia: Fortress Press, 1980.

Mayser, Edwin. *Grammatik der griechischen Papyri aus der Ptolemäerzeit: Mit Einschluss der Gleichzeitigen Ostraka und der in Ägypten Verfassten Inschriften.* Volume 2, part 3. Berlin and Leipzig: Walter de Gruyter and Co., 1934.

Meecham, H. G. "The Imperatival Use of ἵνα in the New Testament." *JTS* 43 (1942): 179-80.

Meeks, Wayne A. *The First Urban Christians: The Social World of the Apostle Paul.* New Haven: Yale University Press, 1983.

Meyer, Lauree Hersch, and Graydon F. Snyder. "Sexuality: Its Social Reality and Theological Understanding in 1 Corinthians 7." Pages 359-70 in *SBL Seminar Papers.* 1981.

Moore, A. L. *The Parousia in the New Testament.* Leiden: E. J. Brill, 1966.

Müller, Ulrich B. *Prophetie und Predigt im Neuen Testament: Formgeschichtliche Untersuchungen zur urchristlichen Prophetie.* SNT 10. Gütersloh: Gütersloher Verlagshaus Gerd Mohn, 1975.

Muraoka, Takamitsu. "The Use of ὡς in the Greek Bible." *NovTest* 7 (1964/1965): 51-72.

Murphy-O'Connor, Jerome. *1 Corinthians.* New Testament Message 10. Wilmington DE: Michael Glazier, Inc., 1979; reprint, 1982.

Murray, Gilbert. *Five Stages of Greek Religion: Studies based on a Course of Lectures Delivered in April 1912 at Columbia University.* Oxford: Clarendon Press, 1925.

Nagel, P. *Die Motivierung der Askese in der Alten Kirche und der Ursprung des Mönchtums.* Berlin: Akadamie Verlag, 1966.

Nickelsburg, George W. E. *Jewish Literature Between the Bible and the Mishnah.* Philadelphia: Fortress Press, 1981.

—————, and Michael E. Stone. *Faith and Piety in Early Judaism: Texts and Documents.* Philadelphia: Fortress Press, 1983.

Niederwimmer, Kurt. *Askese und Mysterium: Über Ehe, Ehescheidung und Eheverzicht in den Anfangen des christlichen Glaubens.* Göttingen: Vanderhoeck & Ruprecht, 1975.

—————. *Der Begriff der Freiheit im Neuen Testament.* Berlin: Alfred Töpelmann, 1966.

Nisbet, Robert. *The Social Philosophers: Community and Conflict in Western Thought.* New York: Thomas Y. Crowell, Inc., 1973.

Nock, A. D. Conversion: *The Old and the New in Religion from Alexander the Great to Augustine of Hippo.* Oxford: Oxford University Press, 1961.

North, Helen. *Sophrosyne.* Ithaca: Cornell University Press, 1966.

Orr, William F., and James Arthur Walther. *1 Corinthians: A New Translation. Introduction with a Study of the Life of Paul, Notes, and Commentary.* Anchor Bible 32. Garden City NY: Doubleday and Company, Inc., 1976.

Painter, John. "Paul and the πνευματικοί at Corinth." Pages 237-50 in *Paul and Paulinism.* Edited by M. D. Hooker and S. G. Wilson. London: SPCK, 1982.

Parker, Robert. *Miasma: Pollution and Purification in Early Greek Religion.* Oxford: The Clarendon Press, 1983.

Perrin, Norman. *The New Testament: An Introduction.* New York: Harcourt Brace Jovanovich, Inc., 1974.

Peters, F. E. *The Harvest of Hellenism: A History of the Near East from Alexander the Great to the Triumph of Christianity.* New York: Simon and Schuster, 1970.

Petersen, Norman R. *Rediscovering Paul: Philemon and the Sociology of Paul's Narrative World*. Philadelphia: Fortress Press, 1985.

Preisker, Herbert. *Das Ethos des Urchristentums*. Gütersloh: C. Bertelsmann, 1949.

Proksch, Otto. ἁγιασμός. *TDNT* 1 (1964) 113-15.

Randall, John Hermann. *Hellenistic Ways of Deliverance and the Making of the Christian Synthesis*. New York: Columbia University Press, 1970.

Reicke, Bo. "Official and Pietistic Elements of Jewish Apocalyptic." *JBL* 79 (1960): 137-50.

Reitzenstein, Richard. *Hellenistic Mystery Religions: Their Basic Ideas and Significance*. Translated by John E. Steely. Pittsburg: The Pickwich Press, 1978.

Rensberger, David. "As the Apostle Teaches: The Development of the Use of Paul's Letters in Second-Century Christianity." Ph.D. dissertation, Yale University, 1981.

Rist, John M., ed. *The Stoics*. Berkeley: University of California Press, 1978.

——————. "The Stoic Concept of Detachment." Pages 259-72 in *The Stoics*. Edited by John M. Rist. Berkeley: University of California Press, 1978.

——————. *Stoic Philosophy*. Cambridge: University Press, 1969.

Robertson, Archibald T., and Alfred Plummer. *A Critical and Exegetical Commentary on the First Epistle of St. Paul to the Corinthians*. International Critical Commentary. Second edition. Edinburgh: T. & T. Clark, 1914; reprint, 1955.

Robinson, James M. "World in Theology and in New Testament Theology." Pages 88-110 in *Soli Deo Gloria: Studies in Honor of William Childs Robinson, Sr*. Edited by J. McDowell Richards. Richmond VA: John Knox Press, 1968.

Robinson, John A. T. *The Body: A Study in Pauline Theology*. Studies in Biblical Theology 5. London: SCM Press, Ltd., 1952; reprint, 1957.

Rollins, Wayne G. "The New Testament and Apocalyptic," *NTS* 17 (1971): 454-76.

Russell, D. S. *The Method and Message of Jewish Apocalyptic: 200 B.C.–A.D. 100*. London: SCM Press, Ltd., 1964.

Sanders, Jack T. *Ethics in the New Testament*. Philadelphia: Fortress Press, 1975.

Sasse, Hermann. κόσμος. *TDNT* 3 (1965) 868-95.

Schade, *Hans-Heinrich. Apokalyptische Christologie bei Paulus: Studien zum Zusammenhang von Christologie und Eschatologie in den Paulusbriefen*. Göttinger Theologische Arbeiten 18. Göttingen: Vandenhoeck & Ruprecht, 1981.

Schmithals, Walter. *Gnosticism in Corinth*. Translated by John E. Steely. Nashville and New York: Abingdon Press, 1971.

Schneider, Johannes. σχῆμα. *TDNT* 7 (1971) 954-58.

Schrage, Wolfgang. *Die konkreten Einzelgebote in der paulinischen Paränese: Ein Beitrag zur neutestamentlichen Ethik*. Gütersloh: Gütersloher Verlagshaus (Gerd Mohn) 1961.

——————. "Die Stellung zur Welt bei Paulus, Epiket und in der Apokalyptik. Ein Beitrag zur 1 Kor. 7, 29-31," *ZThK* 61 (1964): 125-54.

Schulz, Siegfried. "Evangelium und Welt. Hauptprobleme einer Ethik des Neuen Testaments." Pages 483-502 in *Neues Testament und christliche Existenz*. Edited by H. D. Betz and Luise Schottroff. Tübingen: J. C. B. Mohr (Paul Siebeck), 1973.

Schütz, John H. *Paul and the Anatomy of Apostolic Authority*. Cambridge: Cambridge University Press, 1975.

Schweizer, Eduard. "Paul's Christology and Gnosticism." Pages 115-23 in *Paul and Paulinism. Essays in Honour of C. K. Barrett*. Edited by M. D. Hooker and S. G. Wilson. London: SPCK, 1982.

Sevenster, Jan Nicholaas. *Paul and Seneca*. NovTest Suppl. 4. Leiden: E. J. Brill, 1961.

Shires, Henry M. *The Eschatology of Paul in the Light of Modern Scholarship*. Philadelphia: Westminster Press, 1964.

Soelle, Dorothy. *Political Theology*. Translated and with an introduction by John Shelley. Philadelphia: Fortress, 1974.

Ste Croix, G. E. M. de. *The Class Struggle in the Ancient Greek World: From the Archaic Age to the Arab Conquests*. Ithaca: Cornell University Press, 1981.

Stendahl, Krister. "The Apostle Paul and the Introspective Conscience of the West." Pages 78-96 in *Paul Among Jews and Gentiles*. Philadelphia: Fortress Press, 1976.

Stuhlmacher, Peter. "Erwägungen zum Problem von Gegenwart und Zukunft in der paulinischen Eschatologie." *ZThK* 64 (1967): 423-50.

Swain, Joseph Ward. *The Hellenic Origins of Christian Asceticism*. New York: Columbia University Press, 1916.

Theissen, Gerd. *The Social Setting of Pauline Christianity: Essays on Corinth*. Edited and translated with an introduction by John H. Schütz. Philadelphia: Fortress Press, 1982.

Troeltsch, Ernst. *The Social Teachings of the Christian Churches*. Volume 1. Translated by Olive Wyon. Introduction by H. Richard Niebuhr. Chicago: University of Chicago Press, 1931; reprint, 1981.

Unnick, W. C. van. "Die Rucksicht auf die Reaktion der Nicht-Christen als Motiv in der altchristlichen Paränese." In *Judentum, Urchristentum, Kirche: Festschrift für Joachim Jeremias*. Edited by Walther Eltester. Berlin: Verlag Alfred Töpelmann, 1960.

Van der Leeuw, G. *Religion in Essence and Manifestation*. Two volumes. Translated by J. E. Turner. Gloucester MA: Peter Smith, 1967.

Vielhauer, P. "Introduction" (to "Apocalyptic in Early Christianity"). Translated by David Hill. Pages 608-41, volume 2, of *New Testament Apocrypha*. Edited by Wilhelm Schneemelcher. English translation edited by R. McL. Wilson, 608-41. Philadelphia: Westminster Press, 1963.

Walther, James. *1 Corinthians*. Garden City NY: Doubleday and Co., 1976.

Weber, Max. *The Protestant Ethic and the Spirit of Capitalism*. Translated by Talcott Parsons. Introduction by Anthony Giddens. Third edition. New York: Charles Scribner's Sons, 1976.

——————. *The Sociology of Religion*. Translated by Ephraim Fischoff. Boston: Beacon Press, 1963.

Weiss, Johannes. *Der erste Korintherbrief*. KEK 5. Ninth edition. Göttingen: Vandenhoeck & Ruprecht, 1910.

Wenham, David. "The Christian Life: A Life of Tension—A Consideration of the Nature of Christian Experience in Paul." Pages 80-94 in *Pauline Studies: Essays Presented to Professor F. F. Bruce on his 70th Birthday*. Edited by Donald A. Hagner and Murray J. Harris. First American edition. Grand Rapids: Wm. B. Eerdmans Publishing Co., 1980.

Wilson, Bryan R. *Magic and the Millennium: A Sociological Study of Religious Movements of Protest among Tribal and Third-World Peoples*. New York: Harper & Row, Publishers, 1973.

Wilson, R. McL. "Gnosis at Corinth." Pages 102-14 in *Paul and Paulinism*. Edited by M. D. Hooker and S. G. Wilson. London: SPCK, 1982.

Wolbert, Werner. *Ethische Argumentation und Paränese in 1 Kor. 7*. Düsseldorf: Patmos-Verlag, 1981.

Index of Ancient Writings

Old Testament

Genesis
1:28-29 .... 55n23

Esther
1:1 51

Psalms (LXX)
35:8 .... 50n8
54:22 .... 51n13
61:9 .... 50n8
90:4 .... 50n8
107:10 .... 50n8

Proverbs
27:12 .... 51n13

Ecclesiastes
3:5 .... 54n19

Isaiah
32:18 .... 50n8

Jeremiah
46:9-10 .... 25n5
49:11 .... 50n8
50:26-27 .... 25n5

Joel
2:16 .... 54n19
3:14-15 .... 25n15

Obadiah
11 .... 29n24

Zechariah
10:7 .... 29n24

New Testament

Matthew
5:32 .... 19n21
6:31 .... 51n14
10:19 .... 51n14
15:19 .... 18n17
28:14 .... 51n9

Mark
7:21 .... 18n17
10:1-12 .... 19n21
13:19 .... 20n27
13:20 .... 20n14

Luke
16:18 .... 19n21
21:23 .... 19n27
21:34 .... 51n14

Acts
20:28 .... 77n20

Romans
1:7 .... 76n14
1:24 .... 79n44
1:29 .... 80n49
2:25 52
3:26 .... 26n12
5:6 .... 26n12
6 .... 78n28
6:1-11 .... 24n3
8:16 .... 76n16
8:18 .... 26n12
8:21 .... 76n16
8:33 .... 76n12
9:7-8 .... 77n24
9:8 .... 76n16
9:9 .... 26n12
11:5 .... 26n12
12:1-2 .... 79n40
12:9-10 39
12:13-15 39
13 24
13:5 .... 20n27
13:11 .... 26n11
13:11-14 23

1 Corinthians
chs. 1–4 .... 11, 13
1:2 .... 76n11, 77n19
1:16 .... 16n12
1:20-21 .... 78n32
1:26 .... 87n64
1:27 .... 76n12
2:12 .... 78n32
3:16-17 .... 78n38
3:19 .... 78n32
4:5 .... 26n11
4:14 .... 76n16
chs. 5–6 .... 13nn6, 7
5:9 11
5:9-10 81
5:9-11 .... 12, 12n1, 18n17
5:10 .... 78n32
5:10-11 .... 78n36
5:11 .... 78n28
5:12-13 .... 78n31
6:1-8 .... 78n28
6:2 .... 78n32

6:6 .... 78n33
6:9 .... 18n7, 78n36, 80n49
6:11 78
6:12-20 11
ch. 7 ....xi, 5, 6, 7, 12, 13, 17, 21, 22, 28,
      30, 31, 32, 33, 34, 37, 39, 46, 47, 50, 50n6,
      64, 65n61, 69, 71, 82, 83, 84, 85, 86
chs. 7-10 .... 80n48, 83
chs. 7-15 .... 13, 85
chs. 7-16 .... 11, 13
7:1 .... 12nn1, 2, 14n8, 15n11
7:1b 63n56
7:1-7 .... 14, 15, 50
7:1-16 80
7:1-28 65
7:2 .... 18, 18n17, 73
7:5 .... 26n12, 54, 55
7:6 .... 26n8
7:7 .... 15n11, 16
7:7a 17
7:8 ......14n8, 15, 15n9, 15n11, 16n12, 26n8
7:8-9 .... 14, 18n18
7:9 .... 14n8, 18, 18n18
7:10 15
7:10-11 14
7:11 .... 15, 15n9, 16n12, 19n20
7:11b 19
7:12 .... 26n8, 39
7:12-13 .... 52, 78n33
7:12-15 19
7:12-16 14
7:12-24 53
7:13 .... 19n21
7:14 19
7:15 .... 15, 19n21
7:16 81
7:17 .... 15n9, 16n12
7:17-24 .... 14, 15, 21, 21n32, 26n9, 84
7:19 .... 16, 22, 69, 82, 84
7:20 .... 15n9, 16n12
7:21 .... 16, 81
7:24 .... 15nn, 9, 10, 16, 16n12, 25, 26n9
7:25 .... 12n2, 14n8, 22, 49n1
7:25-28 .... 22, 74n1
7:25-35 .... 20n25
7:25-38 14
7:25-40 45
7:26 .... 15, 15n11, 20,
                    20n26, 20n30, 22, 49n1
7:27 .... 15n11, 52
7:28 .... 14n8, 16n12, 17, 20, 20n25,
                    22, 26, 49n1
7:29 .... 21n32, 22, 26, 26n8, 43, 45, 47
7:29a 24, 25, 33, 34, 37, 39, 40,
                    41, 42, 44, 49n1, 50
7:29b 29, 41
7:29-31 .... 7, 8, 20n27, 22, 23, 24, 25,
      30, 32, 34, 36, 38, 39n47, 40, 45, 49n1,
                    68n70, 83, 84, 86, 92
7:29-31a 40, 49nn2, 3, 50, 50n5, 85
7:29-35 .... 7n19, 8, 9, 14, 20n25, 21,
      21n32, 25, 74, 80n48, 83, 84, 86, 87

7:29b-31a 24, 25, 33, 34, 35, 37, 39,
                    42, 44, 45
7:30 43
7:30c 30
7:31 .... 21n32
7:31a 30
7:31b 34, 37, 39n47, 40, 41, 42,
                    43, 44, 47, 50, 78n32
7:31b-35 .... 14, 33, 42, 44, 47
7:32 .... 21n32, 49, 49n1, 50, 50n6, 51, 64
7:32-35 .... 10, 22, 43, 44, 47, 49n2, 50,
                    53, 54, 55, 69, 87, 89, 90
7:32a 64n60
7:32b 50
7:32b-34 .... 21n32
7:33 .... 52, 53
7:33-34 .... 64, 68, 78n32
7:34 .... 50, 52, 53, 56
7:35 .... 52, 68, 69, 70
7:35b 50
7:36 .... 17, 20n25, 74
7:36-38 .... 16, 20n25, 74n1
7:36-40 65
7:37 .... 20n27
7:38 .... 15n11, 18, 22
7:39-40a 14, 18n18
7:40 .... 49n1
7:40a 15n11, 16n12, 20n30, 21
7:40b 12n4, 14, 21, 96
ch. 8 17
8:1 .... 12n2, 80
8:3 .... 76n13
8:5-6 77
8:8 80
9:19-20 39
9:24-27 11
10:1 .... 15n10
10:1-22 .... 11, 78n36
10:15-22 .... 78n28
10:20-21 .... 78n37
10:27 .... 78n33
10:32 .... 77n19
11:2-34 11
11:3 .... 15n11
11:22 .... 77n19
11:29-30 .... 78n28
11:32 .... 78n32
12:1 .... 12n2, 15n10
14:13-14 39
14:22-23 .... 78n33
15:1 .... 15n10
15:9 .... 77n19
15:50 .... 15n10, 45
16:1 .... 12n2
16:12 .... 12n2
16:15 .... 15n10
2 Corinthians
   1:1 ....76n11, 77n19
   1:17 .... 28n22
   3:12 .... 28n22
   4:4 .... 78n33
   6:2 .... 26n11

6:4 .... 20n27
6:4-10 .... 29n24
6:13 .... 76n16
6:14 .... 78n33
6:14-17 .... 78n36
6:14-7:1 11
6:16 .... 78n38
7:1 .... 79n39
7:8 .... 54n21
9:7 .... 20n27
9:18 .... 28n22
12:10 .... 20n27
12:14 .... 76n16
12:21 .... 18n17
13:11 .... 27n17

Galatians
1:13 .... 77n19
2:5 .... 54n21
2:11-14 .... 78n28
3:26-27 .... 78n28
4:3 .... 78n32
4:8 .... 78n34
4:9 .... 76n13
4:19 .... 76n16
4:22-23 .... 77n24
5:1 .... 24n3
5:2 .... 25n7
5:6 52
5:9 .... 80n49
5:14-15 52
5:16 .... 25n7, 79n44
5:19 18
5:20 .... 78n36
5:23 .... 24n3
5:24 .... 79n44
5:25 .... 24n3
6:14 .... 78n32
6:16 .... 77n23

Ephesians
1:1 .... 76n11
1:4 .... 76n12
5:3 .... 18n17
5:5 .... 18n17
5:21-23 .... 15n11

Philippians
1:1 .... 76n11
2:15 .... 77n16, 79n41
3:1 .... 27n17
4:8 .... 27n17

Colossians
1:2 .... 76n11
2:8 .... 78n32
2:20 .... 78n32
3:3-5 .... 24n3
3:5 .... 18n17
3:9-12 .... 24n3
3:12 .... 76, 76n12, 76n14, 79n46
3:18 15
3:19 .... 15n11
4:5 .... 78n31

1 Thess.

1:4 .... 76n14
1:9 77
1:14 .... 76n12
2:17 .... 54n21
3:7 .... 20n27
3:10 86
4:1 .... 27n17
4:3 .... 18n17, 79n45
4:3-8 80
4:5 .... 78n34
4:10b-12 .... 90n73
4:12 .... 78n31
5. 24
5:1 .... 26n11
5:1-11 .... 23, 24
5:2-3 24
5:6-11 24
5:8 .... 79n46
5:22 .... 79n45

2 Thess.
2:13 .... 76n14
3:1 .... 27n17
3:7-12 86

1 Tim.
1:10 .... 18n17
3:5 77
3:16 77
4:8 .... 27n17
5:14 .... 18n18

Titus
2:12 .... 79n44

Philemon
15 .... 54n21

Hebrews
3:6 .... 78n38
4:9 .... 77n26
10:21 .... 78n38
10:30 .... 77n26
13:4 .... 18n17

James
1:27 .... 78n40

1 Peter
1:14 .... 79n39
1:18 .... 24n3
1:22-23 .... 24n3
1 Pet. 2:5 .... 78n38
2:9 .... 77n25
2:11 .... 79n44, 79n45
2:12 .... 79n41
5:7 .... 51n14

2 Peter
3:12 .... 26n14

Revelation
2:14 .... 18n17
2:20 .... 18n17
2:21 .... 18n17
9:21 .... 18n17
18:14 .... 77n26
21:8 .... 18n17, 78n36
22:15 .... 18n17

Other Jewish Writings

Philo:
Leg. All. 2:85............................ 61n44
Spec. Leg. 2.20-21 .... 61n44
    4.88................................. 61n44
Mut. Nom., 32 .... 61n44
Fuga, 38, 63 .... 61n44
Opif. Mund., 144 .... 61n44
    151................................. 61n44
Wisdom
6:15..................................... 50n89
7:23..................................... 50n8
Sirach
6:3-4 .... 79n43
30:24 .... 51n13
38:29 .... 51n13
42:9 .... 51n13
2 Maccabees
6:10..................................... 51n13
4 Maccabees
8:2 .... 50n89
2 Baruch
10:13 .... 20n27
4 Ezra
5.. 24n4
5:1-13 .... 20n27
6:18-24 .... 20n27
9:1-12 .... 20n27
6 Ezra = 4 Ezra 16 .... 24n4, 31
16:35-39 24
16:35-44 .... 24, 31, 46
16:37-39 31
16:40 46
16:40-44 .... 24, 31, 42
16:44 31
16:45-48 .... 46n73, 46
1 Enoch
10....................................... 34n33
48:7 45
2 Enoch
66 .... 34, 34n33
Jubilees
23:11-31 .... 20n27
T. Naph.
8.. 54n19

Other Christian Writings

Ignatius:
Eph. 77
    2:3 .... 79n44
    4:17 .... 79n39
    6:11 .... 79n46
    6:14 .... 79n46

Mg. 77
    7:2 .... 78n38
Tr. 77
Phld. 77
Phld. pr. 77n22
Polyc. 7:1 .... 51n9
Sm. 77
Rom. pr. 79n42
Hermas:
Vis. 1:1, 6 .... 77n20
    3.4 .... 77n20
    3.6, 5 .... 79n44
    3.11, 3 .... 79n44
    4.1, 8 .... 79n46
Sim. 1.3 .... 79n42
    1.11 .... 79n42
    5.5, 3 .... 77n26
    6.1, 2 and 4 .... 79n46
    6.5, 3 .... 79n46
    8. 6, 4 .... 77n20
    8.8, 1-2 .... 79n44
    8.9, 1 .... 79n46
    9.13, 1 .... 77n20
    9.13, 9 .... 78n38
    9.14, 1 78
    9.20, 1-2 .... 79n44
    9.29, 3 .... 79n46
    18.2 77
Mand. 2.2 .... 79n45
    2.3-4 .... 79n46
    5.2, 2 .... 79n44
    5.2.3 .... 51n9
    5.2.8 .... 79n46
    7.3 .... 79n45
    9.7 and 10 .... 79n46
    10.1, 4 .... 79n44
    10.3, 1 and 4 .... 79n46
    11.4 .... 79n46
    11.8 .... 79n45
    12.1, 1 .... 79n46
    12.1, 3 .... 79n45
    12.2, 4 .... 79n46
Barnabas
    4:3 .... 26n14
    7:11 .... 77n20
    14:6 .... 77n25
    16:7 .... 78n35
    20:1 .... 78n36
1 Clement
    pr. 77
    6:3-4 .... 79n43
    14:1-4 .... 77n20
    17:1 .... 78n35
    59:4 .... 77n26
2 Clement
    2-5:1 .... 79n42
    5:6 .... 79n42

Greek and Roman Authors

Aeschylus:
Eum. 132 .... 51n11
Sept. c Theb, 287ff. 51n
Chion of Heraclea:
Ep. 12 .... 88n67
13 .... 88n67
Dio Chrysostom:
Or.20.1-2 60
20.7-8 60
20.26 .... 60, 88n67
Diogenes Laertius:
Lives 6:29 38
7:130 .... 88n67
Epictetus .... (cf. 29)
Diss. 1.29, 59 .... 63n57
2.21, 22 .... 63n57
3 37
3.12.8 .... 61n47
3.13 .... 61n45
3.13, 7-8 .... 61n46
3.13.8 .... 61n47
3.22, 69 .... 63n57
4.1.163 .... 69n72
4.4 .... 61n45
2.21 ....38, 6n41
3.17, 24 .... 38n41
4.1, 4 .... 38n41
Herodotus:
II.135 .... 29n24
IV.81 .... 29n24
IV.99 .... 29n24
IX.42 .... 29n24
Marcus Aurelius:
Meditations 4.3.2-3 .... 61n42
Musonius Rufus (Lutz):
4.22.90 .... 64n58
Pindar:
Olymp. 1, 109:2, 60 .... 51n11
Nem. 3, 69 .... 51n11
Plato:
Apol. 29a 29n24
29.32 .... 51n11
Crat., 414d.1 .... 51n11
Cri., 44c8 .... 51n11
Euphr., 3c5 .... 51n11
Gorgias 517b 29n24

Leg. 9p854E 29n24
XI.917a2 .... 51n11
Phaed. 66bc 58n33
79c 58
79d 58
80 57
Pol. 287a.5 .... 51n11
Rep. I 344e.16 .... 51n11
VIII 563d.8 .... 51n11
Theaet. 173de 57n31
Tim. 27d-28a 57n32
88ab 59n34
Symp. 174D 59n39
211-12 57
220c.7 .... 51n11
Plotinus:
Enn. 1.1.12, 18 .... 62n49
2.3.4.14-15 .... 62n51
Porphyry:
Vit. Plot. 2.17.9 .... 62n48
22 .... 62n48
Seneca:
Ad. Polyb 88n66
De Benef 88n66
De Clem. 88n66
De Tranq. IV.1-6 .... 89n68
EM. 39 88
Ep. 88n66
2.1 .... 60n40
25.6 .... 60n40
28.1 .... 60n40
56.6.7 60
Sextus Empiricus:
Adv. Eth., 117 ....50n7

Sophocles:
Ai. 1207 50
Oed. Tyr., 1124 .... 51n10
1460 .... 51n10
Thucydides:
I.21.1 .... 29n24
II.71 .... 29n24
Xenophon:
Anabasis I.1.13 .... 29n24
V.4.34 .... 29n24
Cyrop. VIII, 7, 112 .... 51n11